D0058570

TURKEY
Hunting Tactics

**Expert Advice for
Locating, Calling and
Decoying Wild Turkeys**

**Creative Publishing
international**

Minneapolis, Minnesota

CREDITS

Creative Publishing international

Copyright © 2001 by Creative Publishing international, Inc.
All rights reserved.

Creative Publishing international, Inc.
400 First Avenue North, Suite 300
Minneapolis, MN 55401
1-800-328-3895
www.creativepub.com
All rights reserved.

President/CEO: Ken Fund
Vice President/Sales & Marketing: Kevin Hamric

TURKEY HUNTING TACTICS

Executive Editor, Outdoor Group: Don Oster
Editorial Director: David R. Maas
Managing Editor: Jill Anderson
Editor: Steven Hauge
Creative Director: Brad Springer
Senior Art Director: David W. Schelitzche
Art Director: Joe Fahey
Photo Researcher: Angela Hartwell
Director, Production Services: Kim Gerber
Production Manager: Helga Thielen
Production Staff: Stephanie Barakos, Laura Hokkanen

Contributing Photographers: Scott Anderson, Mike Biggs, Gary Clancy, Carl R. Sams II /Dembinsky Photo Associates, Laurie Lee Dovey, Jeanne Drake, Gary W. Griffen, Donald M. Jones, Mitch Kezar, Bill Kinney, Lee Kline, Lance Krueger, Wyman Meinzer, Gary Nelson, Bill Thomas, Lovett Williams, Gary Zahm

Printed in U.S.A.
10 9 8 7 6 5

Library of Congress Cataloging-in-Publication Data

Turkey hunting tactics : expert advice for locating, calling, and decoying wild turkeys.

    p. cm. -- (Complete hunter)
    ISBN 0-86573-131-4 (soft cover)
    1. Turkey hunting. I. Creative Publishing International.
II. Complete hunter (Creative Publishing International)
    SK325.T8 T89 2001
    799.2'4645--dc21

                                 00-046867

CONTENTS

INTRODUCTION

THE RESTORATION OF THE WILD TURKEY IN NORTH AMERICA REPRESENTS ONE OF THE GREATEST STORYBOOK COMEBACKS IN THE HISTORY OF WILDLIFE MANAGEMENT. Nearly extinct at the turn of the century, the wild turkey has a current range that exceeds its original native range, thanks to the efforts of wildlife agencies and hunter interest groups. The continuing practice of enlightened management strategies, controlled harvests and restocking efforts means that turkeys will remain plentiful for generations to come.

The popularity of the wild turkey among hunters has grown in proportion to its amazing resurgence. Wherever turkeys have been established in huntable populations, the waiting list for hunting permits has grown steadily. More than 4 million sportsmen hunt turkeys each year.

Turkey Hunting Tactics will introduce you to all aspects of turkey biology and behavior. You'll learn about the four huntable subspecies in the United States: their habitat and food preferences, their growth and development patterns, their special needs for survival. Wild turkeys are legendary for their acute senses, and the reputation is well deserved. You'll develop a new respect for the species' adaptability and toughness as you learn the do's and don'ts that help hunters avoid detection.

Spring breeding time is when toms are most vulnerable to hunters, and understanding this breeding behavior is essential to hunting turkeys successfully. Vocalization, or "turkey talk," becomes the hunter's key skill during the spring season. Our section on calls will acquaint you with all types of calls and explain how to use them to lure old tom into your gun sights.

We cover equipment for hunting turkeys, including

weapons such as shotguns, bows and arrows, and muzzle-loaders. You'll learn how to select the right turkey load, and how to test and pattern the weapon to ensure a clean kill. Blinds, decoys and clothing are shown in detail, including information on how to adapt your setup to changing conditions. A day in the woods can be miserable for the ill-equipped hunter. Our section on accessories helps you select gear that will enhance your comfort and help provide an enjoyable experience.

Prehunt preparation is an essential ingredient for successful turkey hunters. Information gathering – making the right contacts with landowners, scouting, observing daily movements – can be time-consuming work, but these tasks are invaluable to the hunt. Some turkey hunters work at these skills year-round.

Many hunting techniques are explained in this book, including *basic setup and call, spot-and-stalk, float-hunting and tag-team hunting*. The ability to deal with special situations is what separates expert turkey hunters from the rest. We teach you how to deal with problem birds, such as call-shy toms, gobblers in open fields, gobblers with hens or toms hung up by barriers. We also cover hunting in bad weather and have a section on fall hunting.

Once your gobbler has been collected, you'll learn several methods for preserving your trophy. Finally, there is a section showing how to dress and cook a wild turkey. You'll learn several mouth-watering recipes – meals fit for a king.

Written by Gary Clancy, a well-known and respected turkey hunter, *Turkey Hunting Tactics* covers all aspects of turkey hunting, from old, time-tested methods to new, innovative techniques. Whether you're a beginner just starting the sport, or an old veteran of the spring turkey woods, *Turkey Hunting Tactics* will increase your chances for a successful hunt.

Wild Turkey Basics

The wild turkey (*Meleagris gallopavo*), the largest game bird in North America, is related to pheasants, quail and grouse. It is found throughout the United States except for Alaska, and in parts of Canada and Mexico. There are five recognized subspecies, which vary slightly in color and size.

The male wild turkey, called a *tom* or *gobbler*, is a large, robust bird weighing up to 30 pounds and standing as high as 4 feet tall. His body color is brownish black with a metallic, iridescent sheen. The head and neck, nearly bald, vary from white to blue to red. Bright red, fleshy bumps, called *caruncles*, droop from the front and sides of the neck, and a fleshy flap of skin, called a *dewlap*, is attached to the throat and neck. A fingerlike protrusion called a *snood* hangs over the front of the beak. When the tom is alert, the snood constricts and projects vertically as a fleshy bump at the top rear of the beak. A clump of long, coarse hairs, called a *beard*, protrudes from the front of the tom's breast and may grow as long as 12 inches on older birds. Each leg has a spur on it; these spurs are small and rounded on young birds; long, pointed and usually very sharp on mature birds.

The male is called a gobbler for good reason: his rattling, deep-toned call is one of the most recognizable sounds in all of nature. At mating time, toms gobble with full-volume gusto, attempting to attract hens for breeding. Adult males display for hens by fanning their tail feathers, puffing up their body feathers and dragging their wings as they strut. Their heads and necks turn bright red during breeding season or when the tom is otherwise excited.

Adult females, or *hens*, are considerably smaller than toms, rarely weighing more than 10 to 12 pounds. Their overall body color is duller than the male's and lacks his metallic, iridescent sheen. The hen's head and neck are usually blue-gray in color and sparsely covered with small, dark feathers.

CHARACTERISTICS unique to the male wild turkey include: (1) snood, (2) dewlap, (3) caruncles and (4) beard. The female usually lacks these adornments and is duller in overall color than the male.

Caruncles are sometimes present, but smaller than those on toms. Some hens grow small, rudimentary beards and spurs. Although they don't gobble, hens make a variety of cluck, purr, cutt and yelp sounds. Dominant hens may assert themselves with a display resembling that of the male, though they do not strut.

Juvenile birds mature quickly. By their fifth month, the juvenile male *(jake)* and juvenile female *(jenny)* closely resemble adult birds. However, juveniles have darker legs, which turn pink as the birds age. Jakes make feeble gobbles, higher in pitch than the calls of mature toms. Their beards are shorter in length and usually have amber colored tips.

With its powerful legs, the wild turkey is an exceptional runner, and has been clocked at speeds up to 12 mph. Although strong short-distance fliers, turkeys usually run when threatened. When necessary for escape, turkeys launch themselves with a standing leap or a running start and accelerate to 35 mph in a matter of seconds. They cannot remain in the air for more than a few hundred yards, but can glide for a half mile or more when coasting down from a ridgetop.

Subspecies

The five wild turkey subspecies recognized in North America are shown on the following pages. Subspecies can be difficult to distinguish from one another, since regional variations within the group can be more dramatic than physical differences between the subspecies. In addition, where the subspecies' ranges overlap, crossbreeding produces hybrid birds that show traits of both parents. A map showing the current range of all five subspecies (right) is a good starting point in determining where subspecies live.

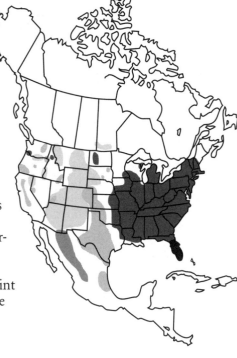

■ *Eastern*   ☐ *Merriam's*   ☐ *Rio Grande*   ■ *Florida*   ■ *Gould's*

10

EASTERN WILD TURKEY
(Meleagris gallopavo silvestris)

The eastern wild turkey can be found through much of the eastern United States, from Maine to North Dakota in the North, and from northern Florida to Texas in the South. Thanks to stocking efforts in the Pacific Northwest, this subspecies thrives today in Washington, Oregon, California and Idaho – areas well beyond its ancestral range. Its range now includes 38 states. With a total United States population estimated between 2.5 and 3 million birds, the eastern turkey is the most abundant of the subspecies – and the most heavily hunted.

The eastern wild turkey is usually found in moist hardwood and pine forests – its Latin name, silvestris, means forest. It favors wooded areas interspersed with open fields, usually with access to water.

The eastern wild turkey is darker than western subspecies. The adult tom is an iridescent dark bronze with black-tipped breast feathers and brown-tipped tail feathers. His wing feathers are barred with black and white in striking contrast to his darker body. The secondary wing feathers, tipped with white, form a whitish triangular area over the rump when the wings are folded.

The hen is lighter in color with brown-tipped feathers on breast and sides.

Because its range extends into cold northern regions, the eastern subspecies tends to grow slightly larger than the western and southern subspecies. Mature eastern toms have been known to weigh as much as 30 pounds.

MERRIAM'S WILD TURKEY
(Meleagris gallopavo merriami)

The Merriam's turkey, named in honor of the first chief of the United States Biological Survey, C. Hart Merriam, originally inhabited Arizona, New Mexico and Colorado, but stocking efforts have extended its range into the Dakotas, Nebraska, Oklahoma and the Pacific Northwest. The total population is estimated at 200,000 to 300,000.

Merriam's turkeys are adaptable birds that inhabit both

11

mountains and open plains, but they are best suited to scrub oak and ponderosa pine foothills. These birds are loosely migratory; they spend summers in the high country and move to lower elevations in winter.

The Merriam's turkey is slightly smaller than the eastern, occasionally growing to weigh as much as 27 pounds. The legs are shorter than those of other subspecies.

The tom's body plumage, slightly darker than that of the eastern turkey, reflects blue, purple and bronze iridescent colors. Its rump feathers and tail tips are light buff to white, much lighter than those on the eastern turkey. This bird is regarded by some as the most beautiful subspecies.

Hens are lighter in color than toms and have breast feathers tipped with buff. The hen's head is sparsely feathered and exhibits more color than that of hens of other subspecies.

RIO GRANDE WILD TURKEY
(Meleagris gallopavo intermedia)

The Rio Grande wild turkey is native to the arid central and southern plains states and northeastern Mexico. The largest numbers are found in Texas, Oklahoma and Kansas, and the bird has been successfully transplanted as far north as the Pacific Northwest. The population in the United States is between 600,000 and 1 million. Its Latin name reflects its appearance midway between the eastern and Merriam's subspecies.

Unlike the forest-dwelling eastern wild turkey, the Rio inhabits open country, near streams or rivers in pine, scrub oak or mesquite forests. Rios range at elevations of up to 6,000 feet. The birds roost in the largest trees available, but where roosting trees are scarce, they roost in small bushes, on power lines and even on oil rigs. Daily movement to and from feeding areas may cover several miles when roost sites and water sources are scarce.

This subspecies is distinguished from the Merriam's by its unusually long legs and copper-colored iridescence. The overall body color is paler than that of the eastern and Florida subspecies. Its tail and rump feathers are tipped with yellowish buff, pink or even tan – lighter in color than the tails of the eastern and Florida subspecies, but darker than the Merriam's. Mature toms can weigh as much as 26 pounds.

FLORIDA WILD TURKEY
(Meleagris gallopavo osceola)

This subspecies derives its Latin title from the name of the legendary Seminole chief, Osceola. Its current and native ranges are entirely within southern Florida, where it favors flat pine woods, oak and palmetto hammocks, and cypress swamp lands. The estimated population is between 75,000 and 100,000 birds.

The Florida wild turkey is a dark bird that closely resembles the eastern wild turkey, although slightly smaller in size. It rarely weighs more than 22 pounds. As compared to the bronze iridescence of the eastern turkey, the Florida turkey's plumage reflects more green and red colors. Its wings are slightly darker than those of the eastern turkey.

GOULD'S WILD TURKEY
(Meleagris gallopavo mexicana)

The Gould's subspecies is found in the mountainous areas of southeastern Arizona and southwestern New Mexico, and in the Sierra Madre Occidental Mountains of northwestern Mexico. Its Latin name is derived from its ancestral range, which was predominantly in Mexico. Gould's turkeys are not legally hunted in the United States, where the total population is estimated at fewer than 1,000 birds. Like other western turkeys, this subspecies favors rocky, mountainous areas; it can be found at elevations up to 10,000 feet.

This bird resembles the Merriam's, but the tips of the tail and rump feathers are whiter. Compared with other subspecies, the Gould's has noticeably longer legs, larger feet and larger central tail feathers. The tom's dark body feathers have a blue-green hue, and the lower back has a greenish gold iridescence. It can weigh up to 30 pounds.

Wild Turkey Habitat

Early explorers reported large numbers of wild turkeys inhabiting the woodlands and plains of North America, but by the early 1900s habitat loss and market hunting had eliminated them from accessible areas. Surviving birds could be found only in a few heavily

timbered regions within the species' original range. By the 1930s and 1940s, it was mistakenly believed that wild turkeys could survive only in dense, remote forests.

In the 1950s, however, as successful trap-and-release techniques were developed, it became clear that turkeys could adapt to many types of habitat. When supported by strict enforcement of game laws, transplanted turkeys readily moved into habitat once thought unsuitable for them.

Today, thanks to the efforts of enlightened game managers, wild turkeys have been established in areas well beyond their original historical range.

MERRIAM'S TURKEYS in western mountain habitat.

GENERAL HABITAT REQUIREMENTS

Wildlife biologists now view wild turkeys as highly adaptable birds. Various subspecies are found in the hardwood forests of the East, the palmetto flats of Florida, the arid mesquite flatlands of Texas, the coniferous mountains of western states – even the prairies of the Dakotas. But regardless of region, wild turkeys require three elements if they are to survive: water, trees and open grassy areas. Turkeys may be found in areas where one or more of these elements is in short supply, but the population is unlikely to flourish.

Throughout most of their range, wild turkeys can survive on the moisture in the foods they eat, but in arid regions they need a regular water source – a spring, seep, stream, lake or even a rancher's stock-watering tank.

Though they spend most of their time on the ground, turkeys require a nighttime roosting location 15 to 20 feet above the ground, where they are safe from predators. Where there are few roosting trees, such as in wetlands or large tracts of cleared land, turkeys are rare. In the West, however, Rio Grande turkeys sometimes roost on manmade structures, such as windmills and oil derricks, if trees are not available.

Turkeys feed, breed and nest in grassy open areas, pastures and fields adjacent to wooded areas. In many regions, these three elements can be found in close proximity. For example, in much of their range, eastern and Florida turkeys are able to find roosting trees, water sources and feeding areas without moving more than a few hundred yards. By contrast, many Rio Grande and Merriam's turkeys travel as many as 5 miles per day to meet these needs.

The presence of the three habitat elements does not guarantee that an area harbors wild turkeys. Heavy predation or adverse climactic conditions limit turkey populations. For example, turkeys have difficulty thriving in far northern areas where heavy snow cover makes it difficult for the birds to move and scratch for food.

Check with state conservation agencies or local chapters of the National Wild Turkey Federation for detailed information on local turkey populations. Scouting (p. 96) is the only sure way to determine if turkeys are present in a specific area.

The effect of human development on wild turkey populations is not yet fully understood. It is possible that turkeys, like white-tailed deer, may adapt well to suburban areas so long as habitat requirements are met.

TYPICAL HABITAT FOR TURKEY SUBSPECIES

EASTERN TURKEY HABITAT in the northern part of the country consists of hardwood forests mixed with grassy openings, farm fields and pastures. Standing water is not essential, but the best turkey habitat is usually well watered by rivers and streams. Eastern turkey habitat in the southern part of the country is a mixture of hardwood and coniferous forests with adjacent pastures, green fields, farm fields or other openings. As in the North, water is not an essential requirement, but the best habitat is usually found relatively close to permanent water.

(continued) *TYPICAL HABITAT FOR TURKEY SUBSPECIES*

*MERRIAM'S TURKEY HABITAT varies and includes hilly grass-
lands mixed with conifers (above), western coniferous mountains (p. 14), prairie cottonwood river bottoms and semiarid
desert sprinkled with pines. The key ingredients are roosting
trees near a water source.*

*RIO GRANDE TURKEY HABITAT consists of prairie grasslands
and savannah mixed with mesquite, live oak, hackberry or
cottonwood trees. The best habitat has roosting areas, either
natural or man-made, in close proximity to water.*

FLORIDA TURKEY HABITAT consists of pine woods and hard-wood hammocks adjacent to cypress ponds and creek bottoms. The majority of turkeys in Florida roost in cypress trees.

GOULD'S TURKEY HABITAT is mainly grassy semiarid mountains mixed with pines and scrub oaks. Large, dominant pines for roosting and a water source, either natural or man-made, are essential.

Age, Growth & Development

Wild turkeys, like other game birds, are fast-growing and fairly short-lived. Individuals living beyond 5 years are considered old. Birds hatched in spring are nearly full grown by fall.

Young turkeys, called poults, weigh about 2 ounces at hatching. Only 30 percent survive their first 2 weeks, which is the most critical period for these young birds. Wild turkeys, like grouse, quail, ducks and geese, are precocial birds that must learn to exhibit adult behavior soon after hatching in order to survive.

The turkey's breeding schedule is timed so poults hatch when forage is at a peak. When the poults begin to hatch, the hen clucks softly to them, beginning the crucial process of imprinting, by which the young birds bond to her. Within a few hours of hatching, poults venture short distances from the nest. Within 12 to 24 hours, they leave the nesting area with the hen.

Within hours of leaving the nest, poults can keep pace with the hen's normal walking pace. They quickly learn to peck at almost anything that moves. In their first summer, young turkeys feed almost exclusively on insects, then slowly switch to seeds, buds, leaves and other plant foods.

JAKES can be distinguished from mature toms by comparing the fanned tail. On jakes (right), the central tail feathers are slightly longer than the surrounding feathers. The tails on mature toms (left) have a smooth sweep.

Poults have yellow down with brown markings when hatched, but within 10 to 12 days, they grow primary wing feathers and can fly short distances. By the end of their first month, when their down has been entirely replaced with plumage, the young birds begin roosting in trees at night. By this time, poults are no longer as dependent on the hen and have adjusted to the adult routine of roosting, feeding, resting and dusting.

By the time they reach their third month in mid- to late summer, young birds are chocolate brown in color and weigh 3 to 4 pounds. The young males, now called jakes, are slightly larger and have longer necks and legs than young females.

During their first fall, at 5 to 6 months of age, jakes weigh 9 to 11 pounds and closely resemble adult hens, which poses difficulty for fall turkey hunters. The best way to identify sex is to examine the head and neck closely. Juvenile males generally have bare skin on the back of the neck and pink to red skin around the eyes and side of the head. Small red *caruncles* may be visible near the base of the neck. Hens usually have blue-gray heads with more feathering on the back of the neck, and rarely have visible caruncles.

By 7 months of age, jakes weigh about 12½ pounds. They are clearly larger than brood hens, which average 8 pounds, and are now darker than hens. They have lost their neck and head feathers, and sport the whitish pink head color typical in adult toms. Small, buttonlike leg spurs and ½- to 2½-inch-long beards are evident on jakes.

At 1 year of age, most juvenile birds have reached sexual maturity. Females generally breed at this age. Young toms, which may weigh in excess of 15 pounds, rarely breed as yearlings due to harassment from aggressive mature toms. Yearlings can be distinguished from older birds by comparing fanned tails. On yearlings, central tail feathers are longer than surrounding feathers. By a tom's second fall, these feathers will be equal in length.

At 2 years of age, wild turkeys have reached full maturity. Legs, brownish pink on juvenile birds, have now become reddish. Toms weigh 21 to 22 pounds on average and have 7- to 9-inch beards still tipped with amber. A few males develop multiple beards. The leg spurs are ¾ to 1 inch long. Some hens develop rudimentary beards, but this is a rare occurrence.

By 3 years of age, the tom's beard has reached its maximum length, about 10 inches long, and the yellow tip has been worn off from dragging on the ground. Leg spurs are about 1¼ inches long and are often curved and sharp. They grow only slightly longer in succeeding years. A healthy adult turkey may live up to 6 years.

Food & Feeding

Wild turkeys are omnivorous. They eat almost anything. This trait, more than any other, accounts for the species' ability to adapt to widely varied habitat. Extensive studies have revealed that turkeys feed on hundreds of different species of plants and animals. A Virginia study of over 500 turkeys conducted during November and December uncovered over 300 species of plants and 300 species of invertebrates in the birds' crops and gizzards.

Within hours of hatching, turkey poults follow the hen into nearby fields and clearings to begin feeding on insects, a protein-rich food source that spurs rapid growth. As they approach 1 month of age, poults begin to adapt to the more varied diet of adult birds. They now require more carbohydrates, which they get from plants and seeds.

Where available, acorns are the favorite food of adult turkeys. They also feed on the nuts and seeds of beech, pine and cedar trees and on the seeds and fruit of flowering shrubs, such as dogwood and sumac. In agricultural areas, turkeys eat oats, corn, wheat, barley, sorghum and sunflowers, though they rarely eat enough to cause substantial crop damage. Insects and other invertebrates are a staple of the turkey's diet.

In spring and early summer, adult birds feed on
the leaves and seeds of grasses and sedges. From summer
through winter, the diet is supplemented with cherries,
grapes, huckleberries and other fruits.

Turkeys typically feed twice each day. In early morning,
birds fly down from tree roosts to feed. In some areas,
they begin foraging directly below roost trees, but in other
areas – the southwestern United States, for example – a
turkey flock may need to move several miles from roosting
trees to find food. In most areas, turkeys can get the water
they require from morning dew or from moisture in the
plants they eat, but in arid country where succulent vegetation is scarce, they need water holes.

After the morning feeding period, the flock moves to cover, where birds dust and loaf until afternoon. Then they feed again, returning to roost just before dark.

Wild turkeys are especially heavy feeders in fall and winter, when they store fat against the rigors of the breeding season. Adult males store fat reserves in the breast "sponge," which is a fatty area above the breastbone. Hens consume snails and other sources of calcium needed to create eggshells.

When food is abundant in spring and summer, birds are on the move constantly, and feeding areas are difficult to pinpoint. A flock may travel 2 mph as it wanders along, feeding on whatever tidbits are available. During fall, however, when turkeys are eating primarily fallen acorns and other nuts, feeding areas are clearly marked by patches of bare earth created when the birds scratch away ground debris.

The ability to survive the harsh conditions of winter proves the wild turkey's toughness. Studies have shown that turkeys can survive extreme cold and heavy snow for up to 2 weeks without food. During these periods, birds conserve energy by minimizing movement and staying on the roost for days at a time. Turkeys may lose half their body weight under such conditions.

Heavy winter snows pose a real risk to turkey survival. Birds find it difficult to move and scratch through deep or crusted snow to find food. In these situations, turkeys often seek areas where deer or cattle have already pawed through the snow. In many northern states, wildlife managers leave fields of standing corn to help turkeys survive severe winters. In the West, livestock feed yards draw huge flocks of wintering turkeys.

Senses

Among devoted turkey hunters, there are countless stories about smart old gobblers who elude hunters for years, until finally outwitted by an expert hunter who, of course, is nothing less than a super woodsman.

Legends aside, wild turkeys are no more intelligent than any other game animal. Nature has, however, provided them with finely developed survival skills. The bird's ability to avoid hunters and other predators stems from an excellent sense of hearing, truly remarkable eyesight and a nervous temperament. Like other game birds, turkeys are pursued

WILD TURKEYS have a field of vision of about 300 degrees, thanks in part to eyes mounted on opposite sides of the head.

by predators – winged, two-legged and four-legged. One of the first things poults learn from their mothers is to fear and flee any unusual movement or sound.

Like most birds, turkeys have poorly developed senses of taste and smell. They make up for this with a nervous temperament, or "wildness." Wild turkeys are always on edge, always alert for danger.

SIGHT.

With eyes set on the sides of its head, a wild turkey can see a 300-degree arc without moving its head. The bird's eyesight is monocular, not binocular. This gives the turkey a nearly full picture of its surroundings at all times. By contrast, a human must turn his head nearly in a complete circle to see the same view. More than any other trait, the ability to instantly spot faint movements makes the wild turkey one of our most challenging game animals. Fortunately for hunters, these birds are not equally adept at judging depth and distance. They often have trouble landing in trees and distinguishing shapes – a weakness that allows a camouflaged hunter to remain virtually undetectable so long as he remains motionless.

Wild turkeys are *diurnal* (active in daylight). They have poor night vision and are vulnerable to night-feeding predators, so they always seek an elevated night roost where they remain until there is sufficient morning light to safely fly down.

HEARING.

Hunters who have seen wild turkeys flee at the slightest noises will testify to the species' acute hearing, but there is no definitive scientific research to verify the bird's hearing capabilities. Since they communicate vocally throughout their lives, the acute hearing is obviously important. In all likelihood they hear only slightly better than do humans. The big difference is that they become instantly alert to unusual noises. They are programmed to pick out unnatural, potentially dangerous sounds. The turkey's ears have no flaps to gather sound; it pinpoints sound direction by quickly turning its head back and forth.

Breeding & Nesting

Fortunately for hunters, the wild turkey's breeding behavior is a noisy, boisterous affair. During spring, mature toms gobble loudly, announcing their presence to any hens and hunters within earshot. When a tom hears the seductive yelps of a hen – or a calling hunter – he often responds swiftly, following where his hormones lead.

The wild turkey's breeding season begins when the longer days of spring prompt an increase in the secretion of sex

hormones. The courtship can start as early as February in the South, can last into late May in the far northern states, and may be delayed or advanced by major weather changes. Increased gobbling marks the start of this annual courtship ritual.

Tom flocks remain intact through the mating season. The dominant tom does most of the breeding and aggressively suppresses the breeding activity of subdominant toms. Hen flocks break into smaller groups of two to five birds as the breeding season progresses. Bred hens eventually seek isolation for nesting.

Once a tom's gobble has been answered by a hen, the two communicate through a series of back-and-forth gobbles and yelps that help them find one another. Once a gobbler

DESPITE the visual drama and the tom's physical dominance, the hen decides if and when mating occurs.

spots a hen, he generally stops his approach and gobbling and immediately begins displaying. It is the hen's responsibility to move closer if she wishes to be bred. If several hens are present, this courtship display may continue for hours.

The highly coordinated strut begins with the tom fanning his tail and puffing his body feathers. He pulls his head back against his chest, drags his wing tips on the ground, and moves forward in a slow, purposeful, stiff-legged walk. He takes three or four steps, then pirouettes. This routine is performed over and over. The performance ends when the tom assumes a normal walking posture with his tail lowered and unfanned. Throughout the strut the tom vibrates his wings, making a low-pitched humming sound, called *drumming*. His head color varies from white to blue to red, depending on his level of excitement.

Despite this visual drama and a tom's physical dominance, the hen decides if and when mating occurs. After approaching the strutting male, a ready female flexes her neck against her back, holds her body in a horizontal position and walks in front of him. She then crouches on the ground, inviting the tom to breed her.

A dominant tom who has found a group of hens mates with those that invite him. Subdominant toms manage to breed other hens while the dominant tom is occupied. When a tom is courting females, it's almost impossible for a hunter to call him away. Late in the day, however, as available hens are bred or leave to nest, the tom may again become vulnerable to a hunter's calling.

In late spring, after most hens have been bred and are setting eggs, toms increase gobbling in an attempt to attract any remaining receptive hens; this is a prime time to call one to the gun.

A hen may continue to breed for several days after she begins laying, but she withdraws from the company of toms and other hens when her clutch of eggs is complete and she begins to incubate.

A hen typically chooses a secluded ground nesting site within a few hundred yards of water and hidden against a rock, tree, log or cut bank. Such a location guards a hen's back while she watches for predators approaching from the front.

The nest is little more than a depression in the ground. The hen lays one egg a day, until she has a clutch of 10 to 12. Only when it is complete does she begin incubating. When she first begins laying, the hen spends most of her time away from the nest, hiding the eggs under leaves and debris. She may socialize with other hens and continue to breed at this time, but far from the nest.

Once she begins to incubate, the hen moves off the nest once each day for 1 to 2 hours to eat and drink, and once each hour to turn the eggs. The eggs hatch in about 28 days, all the chicks emerging within 24 to 48 hours.

The majority of first-year hens breed or attempt to breed, except for the Merriam's. For some unknown reason, many Merriam's hens skip their first year. Most mature hens return to the same nesting spot year after year. First-year hens wander widely to find unoccupied territory for their nesting sites. This dispersal behavior is the primary mechanism for the spread of turkeys into new areas. Studies have shown that an established turkey population can expand its range by about 5 miles per year.

Social Behavior & Communication

mong the most social of all game birds, wild turkeys spend much of their time in flocks, dispersing only for a few weeks during the spring nesting season. Though flocks numbering in the hundreds have been observed, most groups contain between 5 and 20 birds. Turkeys follow a complex hierarchical social structure, as shown by the makeup of their flocks.

FLOCK STRUCTURE

For much of the year, a wild turkey population is divided into four types of flocks organized according to gender, age and dominance.

One flock consists solely of mature males. These birds rarely associate with other turkeys except during breeding season. The second flock consists of mature hens who either did not breed or lost their brood. The third flock includes breeding hens and their offspring. In summer, several hens and their offspring may join to form a larger flock. This group stays intact until late fall when the young males, or jakes, leave to form a fourth group. Less mature male poults may remain with the family flock until they feel confident enough to join a jake flock. Turkeys remain in these flocks until lengthening daylight marks the onset of the spring breeding season.

Spring brings on real competition among toms. Although turkeys are not territorial, they do fight to determine hierarchy within the flock. In anticipation of the mating period, toms tussle and fight until a dominant bird emerges as the one who does most of the breeding.

Stimulated by rising hormones, some jakes attempt to join flocks of adult males. Most are rejected, but persistent youngsters may gain acceptance. These youngsters, traveling along the fringes of a mature tom flock, are known as *apprentices*.

As spring breeding progresses, hen flocks break into smaller groups of two to five birds. These gradually disperse as individual females breed and move to isolated nesting sites. Toms try to stay with these small bands of hens.

SOCIAL HIERARCHY

Every turkey flock has a hierarchical structure established and maintained through dominance fights between individuals.

A dominance fight begins when two birds face off at close range and utter warning sounds. The combatants then entangle necks and bite heads. The loser surrenders by breaking free and running away.

TWO TOMS fight for dominance.

High-ranking subordinate turkeys remain alert to opportunities to challenge a dominant bird at any sign of weakness. A dominant tom wounded by a predator, for example, may be attacked by other males looking to improve their positions in the flock hierarchy. This is why subdominant birds often jump on a shot tom.

In addition to individual dominance struggles, entire flocks may vie for dominance. The motivation for these group struggles is not known, since the losing flock is not forced to leave the territory.

COMMUNICATION

The subtleties of turkey communication are not fully understood, though a good deal is known about the calls useful to hunters. Wild turkeys use a vocabulary of nearly 30 sounds, according to some studies. Those most important to hunters are discussed below.

GOBBLE. Mature toms make this namesake call during the spring breeding season, to attract hens. Jakes may gobble, but the sound is low in volume and high in pitch. Toms gobble in response to a hen's *yelp, cutt* or *purr*, and often call spontaneously. A tom usually greets each spring dawn with vigorous, repeated gobbling before flying down from his roost. He may also gobble after returning to his evening roost. The sound is a coarse, booming "gubble-gubble-gubble" and can be heard from a mile away on a still morning.

YELP. Turkeys use this high-pitched "yap, yap, yap" call in a variety of situations with many variations in volume and pitch. Because hens yelp to answer gobbling toms during the breeding season, the yelp is the call most often mimicked by hunters. Yelps are also used to call a dispersed flock together. Hens yelp in response to a peeping poult. Hens on the roost may yelp softly before flying down in the morning.

PURR. This high-pitched, low-volume, quavering call resembles the purring of a cat and indicates a contented bird. Undisturbed adults often purr when feeding or roosting. If the intensity of the purring rises to a louder "PURRRT" call, it indicates slight alarm, and may be followed by an *alarm putt* if danger is detected. Battling toms purr aggressively.

CUTT. The cutt is a series of short, demanding, stacatto "buck buck buck" sounds resembling the excited clucking of a barnyard chicken. Adult turkeys cutt when trying to locate one another or their broods.The cutt is useful to a hunter trying to get a reply from a distant turkey, or attempting to call a quiet tom.

ALARM PUTT. This is a loud, sharp, one-syllable cutt that serves as a warning call. One putt puts other turkeys on full alert. Two will drive them into full flight. A hunter who hears this call is about to lose any chance at a shot.

KEE KEE. This is the call heard when a lost poult seeks its mother or when an adult bird is desperate to rejoin its flock. The call resembles a repeated, high-pitched whistle. In fall, a hunter can use this call to lure a scattered group of turkeys toward him.

Restoration & Conservation

The restoration of wild turkey populations in North America is one of the most significant success stories in the history of wildlife management. From virtual extinction in the early 1900s, the species now numbers approximately 4 million in the United States. Wild turkeys are currently found in every state except Alaska – a vastly wider range than the species occupied in the 19th century. Both the population and range are expected to continue growing.

WILD TURKEYS have a field of vision of about 300 degrees, thanks in part to eyes mounted on opposite sides of the head.

Wild turkeys were plentiful in Colonial times, but habitat loss, combined with unlimited harvests by market hunters through the 1800s, nearly eliminated the birds from most of the United States. The first attempted turkey stocking dates back to 1912, but widespread success was not possible until a wave of wildlife management improvements occurred in the 1930s.

The startling success of turkey restoration is due in large part to the combined efforts of federal and state agencies and sportsmen's groups. The Target 2000 program, for example, was a long-term restoration effort sponsored by the nonprofit National Wild Turkey Federation in cooperation with private sportsmen's groups and government agencies. Target 2000 was a resounding success and worked to stock wild turkeys in an additional 60 million acres of suitable habitat by the year 2000. Today, at least 18 states have completed their wild turkey restoration programs.

Ironically, the same bait-hunting techniques used by market hunters to drive turkeys near extinction are now used by conservation groups to trap birds for relocation. Old-time market hunters typically set out long lines of feed to lure in a large group of turkeys, then took a stand at one end of the line. After a large number of birds arrived and began to feed in a convenient row, the hunters opened fire. Today's bait-lines operate much the same way, except birds are netted rather than shot. Then they are transported to new habitat and released. The cost of capturing, transporting and releasing wild turkeys is estimated at $300 to $500 per bird.

Early efforts to use wild turkeys raised on game farms in restoration efforts proved disastrous. Pen-raised turkeys did not survive in the wild because they lacked survival skills. They often carried diseases that not only killed them, but could be transmitted to true wild stock. In current stocking efforts, wildlife managers release only trapped wild turkeys and only in areas where no turkeys are found.

A turkey-stocking project typically takes about 5 years to generate a stable, huntable population. A ratio of four hens to one tom is released into suitable habitat. Within about 3 years, the population usually increases by 400 to 500 percent, and the range of the new population expands from young hens moving into new territory. This gradual range expansion follows stream beds, valleys and natural breaks in the terrain, and continues until birds encounter a formidable barrier, such as a large river or area of dense human development. Hunting seasons are not opened until a healthy population becomes established.

CONSERVATION

As restoration efforts near completion in many states, wildlife managers turn their attention to monitoring and maintaining established populations and improving the quality of hunting.

Managing wild turkeys, as with any game animal population, is a matter of keeping a balance between the species' reproductive capacity and the factors that limit that capacity – factors such as habitat loss, weather, disease, predation and hunter harvest.

Although uncontrolled hunting once reduced turkey numbers, well-controlled hunting seasons today have little effect on long-term population trends. In reality, hunters and the National Wild Turkey Federation are largely responsible for the resurgence of the wild turkey population, since their license fees and fundraisers have provided most of the funds needed for trap-and-release stocking programs. In some regions, however, poaching can be a problem.

The trend toward spring wild turkey seasons and away from fall seasons has been an important step in controlling hunter harvest. Spring seasons allow only toms to be taken, which ensures the survival of breeding hens. Fall seasons are still allowed in most states, but are structured so that no more than 10 percent of the total population is taken. One Midwest study showed that harvesting 30 percent of male birds during the spring season and 10 percent of all birds during the fall season had no negative effects on long-term wild turkey numbers.

Other methods of controlling hunter harvest include setting strict bag limits, limiting shooting hours, banning certain weapons and ammunition, and restricting the use of decoys and blinds.

Although turkey populations and reproductive rates can

be affected by harsh winters, drought and other environmental factors, the wild turkey has proven to be a tough bird with excellent survival skills. Much wild turkey management effort now focuses on acquiring, preserving and improving habitat suitable for wild turkey.

Wildlife agencies acquire land through purchase or long-term lease. In some states, much of the land available for turkey hunting is owned or leased by the state for the benefit of sportsmen.

To preserve and improve wild turkey habitat, wildlife managers use a variety of strategies. On leased lands where logging is allowed, restricting harvests to no more than 50 percent of the mature trees can ensure the survival of a wild turkey population. In other areas, planting nut producing trees like oaks and chestnuts greatly improves habitat. In densely forested areas, small clear-cut areas provide turkeys with grassy open areas essential for feeding and breeding. Controlled burns help keep forest understories at levels favorable to wild turkeys. Developing water sources and planting grains, grasses and other food crops also promote strong turkey populations.

Hunters and private landowners wishing to establish or enhance habitat for wild turkeys should contact state wildlife agencies for detailed information and advice on how to coordinate efforts. The remarkable ongoing restoration of the wild turkey in North America is due to the tireless, focused efforts of The National Wild Turkey Federation, wildlife managers, numerous agencies and organizations – and to thousands of dedicated hunters.

Shotguns & Ammunition

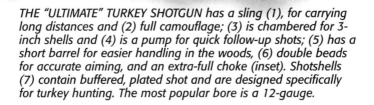

THE "ULTIMATE" TURKEY SHOTGUN has a sling (1), for carrying long distances and (2) full camouflage; (3) is chambered for 3-inch shells and (4) is a pump for quick follow-up shots; (5) has a short barrel for easier handling in the woods, (6) double beads for accurate aiming, and an extra-full choke (inset). Shotshells (7) contain buffered, plated shot and are designed specifically for turkey hunting. The most popular bore is a 12-gauge.

Shotguns loaded with birdshot are the tools of choice for turkey hunters, accounting for more than 90 percent of all birds taken. Since the turkey's heavy wing feathers and thick breast muscles are difficult to penetrate, hunters don't attempt body shots, but aim for the head and neck.

A 12-gauge pump-action or semi-automatic is the most popular gun, because it is relatively light and allows the hunter a quick follow-up shot. A few hunters prefer single-shot or double-barrel guns, and some opt for the 10-gauge,

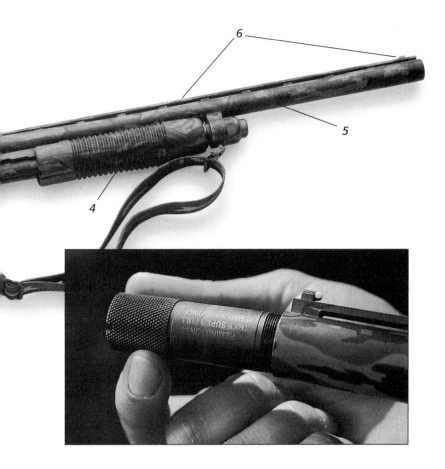

which delivers more shot than a 12-gauge. A 10-gauge is heavy and cumbersome, however, and is not necessary to ensure clean kills at reasonable ranges. Most sportsmen hunt harder and longer with a lighter pump-action or semi-automatic 12-gauge, weighing 7$1/2$ to 8$1/2$ pounds.

BARRELS. Twenty-two to 26-inch barrels handle best in thick turkey habitats. Short barrels reduce weight without sacrificing performance.

Fixed-choke guns should have full chokes to provide the tight pattern necessary for killing head shots. Barrels threaded to accept interchangeable choke tubes can be fitted with "extra-full " or "turkey" chokes designed expressly for turkey hunting. This type of choke delivers the tightest possible pattern. A competent gunsmith can thread the barrel of nearly any shotgun to accept interchangeable chokes. A word of warning: These extra-tight chokes are intended for use with lead shot only; shooting steel shot can easily damage the choke or barrel.

CHAMBER LENGTH. A 12-gauge with 3-inch chamber is ideal for turkey hunting. The 3½-inch 12-gauge delivers a heavier payload, but recoil is punishing, especially in lightweight guns. A 12-gauge with a 2¾-inch chamber also makes a fine turkey gun, putting plenty of shot in the kill zone when used with 1½ or 1⅝ ounces of buffered, plated shot.

FINISH. Because turkeys are sharp-eyed and extremely cautious, the glint from a blued barrel or polished wood stock will spook them. Experienced hunters typically dull their turkey shotguns from muzzle to butt plate with camouflage tape, flat paint or a gun sock. Tape and paint are better than gun socks, which often slip around to cover up the action, trigger, safety or front bead at the worst moments. Most modern turkey guns are sold with dull or full-camouflage finishes.

SIGHTS. Double beads, one on the end of the barrel and another in the middle, are better for aiming a turkey shotgun than are single beads. Lining up two beads forces you to get down on the stock and ensures that you will not shoot over the turkey, a common problem when using a single-bead sight. Some hunters prefer to install rifle-style open sights or peep sights on their turkey shotguns, and others are switching to 1.5x or 2x low-power scopes.

AMMUNITION. For years, turkey hunters have clamored for harder-hitting shot shells. Manufacturers have responded with magnum loads designed specifically for turkey hunting. Most hunters depend upon heavy loads of number 4, 5 or 6 shot pushed by a large powder charge. Buffered loads of nickel or copper-plated shot pattern best because the buffering agent and hard shot reduce "flyers," deformed pellets that plane off course.

ACCESSORIES. Many turkey hunters equip their shotguns with slings, which eases the burden of carrying a gun around all day. Most slings are adjustable and can be removed from the gun, if necessary.

SHOTGUN SIGHTS

SINGLE-BEAD SIGHTS are adequate if you keep your cheek on the stock until you see only the bead over the receiver. If you see the barrel (arrow), the shot will be high.

DOUBLE-BEAD SIGHTS feature a second bead halfway up the barrel. When the rear bead is aligned with the front bead (arrow), you will be on target.

SHOT PATTERN EFFECTIVENESS AT DIFFERENT RANGES

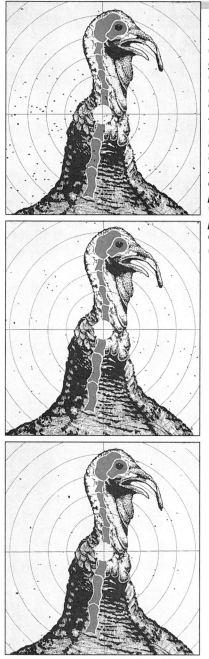

EXTRA-FULL CHOKES, sometimes called turkey chokes, ensure that your gun's pattern is dense enough for killing shots out to 40 yards. Studies have shown that at least 3 pellets must hit the vitals (shaded) of a turkey's head and neck to guarantee a kill. Test-firing the same load at 25 yards with an extra-full choke (top) places 12 pellets in the vitals. Full choke (center) places 6 pellets in the critical area; modified choke (bottom), only 2 pellets.

TURKEY SHOTSHELL LOADS

SIZE OF SHELL	MUZZLE VELOCITY (feet per second)	SIZE OF SHOT	NUMBER OF PELLETS
10-ga. 3½-INCH (2¼ ounces of shot)	1210	4	304
		–	–
		6	506
12-ga. 2¾-inch (1⅝ ounces of shot)	1250	4	219
		5	276
		6	366
12-ga. 3-inch (2 ounces of shot)	1175	4	270
		5	340
		6	450
12-ga. 3½-inch (2¼ ounces of shot)	1150	4	304
		5	382
		6	506
20-ga. 3-inch (1¼ ounces of shot)	1185	4	169
		–	–
		6	281
20-ga. 2¾-inch (1⅛ ounces of shot)	1175	4	152
		–	–
		6	253

Muzzleloaders & Ammunition

Over the past decade, turkey hunters looking to add even more challenge to an already demanding sport have turned to muzzleloading shotguns. Until recently, these weren't ideal for turkey hunting; the cylinder-bore barrels common to most muzzleloading shotguns simply didn't produce a tight enough pattern to ensure clean kills.

Today, however, most manufacturers of muzzleloading shotguns offer either fixed full-choke barrels or inter-changeable choke systems that accept extra-full, screw-in chokes.

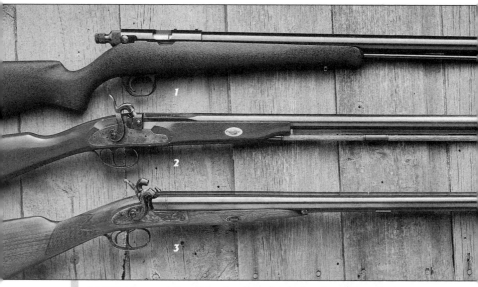

POPULAR muzzleloading shotguns for turkey hunting include: (1) in-line percussion caplock, (2) traditional percussion caplock and (3) double-barreled percussion caplock.

In effective range and firepower, even the best muzzle-loading shotguns can't compete with a modern-day "turkey special" 12-gauge shotgun with semi-automatic or pump action. Nevertheless, growing numbers of hunters willingly accept the difficulties of muzzleloading in exchange for the satisfaction of a time-honored hunting experience.

MUZZLELOADING GUNS. While a few hunters use flint-locks, most prefer the additional reliability of a 12-gauge caplock. These guns, which use a percussion cap to detonate the powder charge, are reliable even in damp weather. For versatility, select a gun that accepts interchangeable chokes. With a full or extra-full choke in place, you're ready for turkeys. Double-barrel muzzleloading shotguns offer the turkey hunter the advantage of a quick follow-up shot, but require special safety precautions. After firing one barrel, always remove the percussion cap from the nipple on the loaded barrel before reloading the empty barrel. And get in the habit of tamping down the load in the unfired barrel just to make sure that the recoil has not created a gap between powder charge and shot. To ensure that you don't charge the same barrel twice, cut a notch into your ramrod at the muzzle when the ramrod is resting on a full charge. Thereafter, if the ramrod mark drops below the muzzle, that barrel is unloaded. If it rests at the muzzle, the gun is already loaded. DO NOT load it again.

AMMUNITION COMPONENTS. To build a turkey-hunting load, you will need five components: powder, shot cups, shot, over-shot wads and percussion caps. The first step is to determine the manufacturer's recommended maximum powder load for your shotgun, as specified in the manufacturer's literature. Pyrodex RS or blackpowder in either FFg or Fg granulation may be used in most modern muzzleloading shotguns. Many hunters assume that the maximum allowed powder charge is best, but this is not always the case, since many muzzleloading shotguns perform best with powder loads well below the maximum. Swapping velocity for pattern density is always a wise trade. The only way to determine the best load for your gun is to experiment with different combinations of shot and powder, while never exceeding the maximum recommended load. If you are unsure of the maximum recommended load for your shotgun, contact the manufacturer.

VOLUME-TO-VOLUME LOADING means measuring an equal volume of both shot and powder, not an equal weight.

The easiest technique to use when determining the most effective load is the volume-to-volume method. This means that one measure can be used for both shot and powder. For example, a powder measure (above) set at 50 grains is used first for measuring the powder charge, then the shot. This gives you the same volume of both components, not the same weight.

QUICK TIP: Quickloads carry premeasured volumes of shot and powder, making for fast, efficient loading in the field, in case a follow-up shot is needed. Quickloads reduce the amount of reloading gear a hunter needs to carry.

There are several wad combinations that may be used in muzzleloading shotguns, but the most efficient is a modern plastic shot cup and a single Styrofoam® or cardboard over-shot wad.

The finest muzzleloading shotgun meticulously loaded with the best components cannot be expected to match a modern, turkey-special shotgun in downrange pattern density. Part of the challenge of hunting with a muzzleloading shotgun is pulling that gobbler in close for the shot. Pattern your muzzleloading shotgun at 25 yards, the ideal range at which to take your shot.

HOW TO LOAD A MUZZLELOADING SHOTGUN

FIRE a couple of percussion caps to make sure the nipple is clear. You should hear a dull "whump," not a sharp "crack," if there are no obstructions.

TILT the muzzle away from your face to avoid injury in case of accidental discharge. Pour the premeasured powder charge down the barrel.

TAMP the plastic shot cup firmly down on top of the powder. If your gun has a screw-in choke, remove it first.

POUR the premeasured volume of shot from the opposite end of the quickload.

INSERT an over-shot wad by pushing it down the barrel until it rests on top the pellets. Replace the screw-in choke.

PLACE a percussion cap on the nipple, and make sure your safety is engaged. The shotgun is now ready to fire.

Rifles & Ammunition

Where wild turkeys may be hunted with rifles as well as shotguns, so called "deer rifles" account for most of the birds taken by riflemen. But unless the hunter is an excellent marksman capable of making head shots at long range, the turkey, struck in the body with the trusty old "ought-six," is often rendered both dead and inedible at the moment of impact. Serious riflemen prefer accurate rifles chambered for smaller calibers, such as the .243 Winchester, .22-250 Remington and .223 Remington. With careful hand-loading, hunters can design loads that maintain excellent accuracy at ranges under 200 yards, while reducing velocity to levels that minimize meat damage.

The little .17 Remington has acquired a large following among rifle turkey hunters. The tiny 25-grain bullet kills turkeys quickly and destroys little meat. Another longtime favorite is the .22 Winchester Rimfire Magnum. At ranges under 100 yards, the .22 mag is potent turkey medicine.

Most serious turkey hunters consider rifles both unsporting and dangerous for turkey hunting.

Bows & Arrows

COMPOUND BOWS are preferred by most turkey hunters because let-off, usually 60 to 80 percent, allows a hunter to hold at full draw longer than possible with traditional bows.

Arrowing a gobbler is one of the toughest challenges for a turkey hunter. Coaxing this nervous, sharp-eyed bird within the 20- to 25-yard range needed for a killing shot requires exceptional patience and excellent calling skills. Then the hunter must come to full draw, and place the arrow into a very small vital area.

A standard deer-hunting bow is suitable for hunting turkeys. If your bow does not have factory camouflage, cover it with camouflage tape. You may want to lower the draw weight of a compound bow to make it easier to hold at full draw for long periods. Often, when bow-hunting turkeys, there is a substantial time lapse between drawing and shooting.

If legal in your area, use a blind and one or more turkey decoys. A blind will help cover the motion of your draw. Decoys lure gobblers close and deflect their attention away from the hunter, often providing the critical extra seconds needed to get off a good shot.

Because an archer needs both hands to shoot, most bowhunters use diaphragm calls (p. 84) for bringing gobblers in close. Quiet clucks and contented purring are best for getting a gobbler to take those last few steps.

Broadheads should have a large cutting diameter. Grabbers retard penetration and increase the odds of the broadhead staying in the bird.

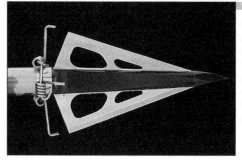

BROADHEADS should have a large cutting diameter. Grabbers retard penetration and increase the odds of the broadhead staying in the bird.

SHOT PLACEMENT FOR BOWHUNTING

SHOT PLACEMENT is crucial when bowhunting gobblers because their vital area is so small. Dashed lines (white) indicate the killing zone for different postures: (1) breast-on

56

strutting tom, (2) breast-on erect bird, (3) facing-away strutting bird, (4) facing-away erect or walking bird, (5) broadside strutting tom and (6) broadside erect bird.

Blinds

Blinds are not essential for most turkey hunting, but can make the difference between success and failure in certain scenarios. A blind covers a bowhunter's motion as he draws to shoot, and hides a gun hunter in an exposed location or in one hunting site for a long period. Blinds are also an asset when introducing young, sometimes antsy, hunters to the sport.

Blinds come in many forms, from simple, natural designs assembled from vegetation to high-tech camouflage tents using elaborate camouflage patterns. But higher cost does not necessarily mean a better blind. Some of the best blinds are also among the simplest; many can be made at little cost.

TYPES OF BLINDS

NATURAL BLINDS assembled from branches, brush or other surrounding vegetation are easy to build. Cut vegetation with small, ratchet-type pruning shears. When assembling your blind, make sure there is enough room to raise and move your bow or gun freely. If your blind is not constructed against a large tree or other solid object, drape burlap or camouflage cloth over the rear of the blind so a turkey approaching from the rear won't detect movement.

ACCORDION BLINDS, made of heavy-duty cardboard, fold up easily to be carried under your arm. It is best to shoot bows around the ends of the blind.

WRAP-AND-STAKE BLINDS are lightweight and portable. A sheet of camouflage material, 3 to 4 feet high and 8 to 12 feet long, is attached to stakes, which are pushed into the ground.

STUMP BLINDS are not as portable as other blinds, but provide protection from the elements and excellent concealment. Stump blinds are not suitable for bowhunting because there is not room to draw.

PYRAMID BLINDS conceal hand and leg movement, are lightweight and easy to assemble. They are most comfortable when used with a backrest.

TENT BLINDS are ideal in places turkeys frequent regularly or where there is little cover. The best blinds are big enough to allow the hunter to sit comfortably and shoot from a sitting or kneeling position. There should be multiple openings for viewing and shooting.

UMBRELLA BLINDS can be made from any large, sturdy umbrella. Spray the top and bottom a flat brown, green and black. Cover the handle with camouflage tape. Umbrellas hide a hunter and can offer protection from the elements.

Decoys

A well-positioned turkey decoy is often the final touch needed to lure a shy tom into shooting range. Especially in open country, toms responding to a hen call may grow suspicious if they can't spot the source of the call. But if they see a decoy, the reassured gobblers often commit and waltz into range. A decoy can work wonders on hard-hunted birds, which tend to be leery of even the best calling.

Decoys can also encourage a turkey to stay within range for extended periods – an asset for bowhunters. By holding a gobbler's attention, a decoy makes it easier to raise your bow or gun without being detected.

Decoys have drawbacks, however. Some are cumbersome to carry. Some blow over in strong winds and look unnatural.

Any decoy may draw the fire of inexperienced or careless hunters. Always position your decoy so that you can see well beyond it. If you see a hunter sneaking toward your decoy, yell to him in a loud voice. Never wave to get his attention. And never use decoys during the fall season when both sexes are legal. Carry decoys in orange safety sacks or tie orange ribbons to them.

It is possible to become too dependent on decoys. Some hunters become so preoccupied with positioning decoys that they spook approaching turkeys. If you can see a gobbler or hear one closing fast, don't bother with a decoy – just sit down against a tree, trust your calling and prepare for the shot.

Motion is often critical to success. Decoys that sway seductively in the slightest breeze or move when jerked with a string can be deadly.

> QUICK TIP: Position a jake decoy closer to you than the hen. A tom will usually bypass the hen to drive the jake away.

Not all states allow the use of decoys, so always check local regulations before using them.

JAKE DECOY STYLES include: collapsible foam in (1) full strut, (2) half-strut and (3) erect position; and (4) folding shell in erect position.

HEN DECOY STYLES include: (1) collapsible foam; (2) folding shell; (3) silhouette; (4) full body; (5) hen with safety orange head, which is both safe and often aggravates toms and (6) motion decoy, which allows the hunter to move the head of the decoy by pulling on a long string.

Clothing

Choosing the proper clothing and footwear ensures comfort under all conditions and increases the odds of successfully bagging a bird.

BOOTS. A turkey hunter will encounter variable weather, habitats and terrain. No single boot is ideal for all situations. In spring, when temperatures can climb to the 70s and 80s, a non-insulated leather or leather-Cordura® combination boot is most comfortable. In arid regions, where cactus spines may puncture Cordura, all-leather boots are best. In colder weather, choose insulated leather or leather-Cordura boots. For walking through mud, wet grass, swamps or creeks, choose boots lined with Gore-Tex® or Cambrelle® material that passes perspiration vapor out, but doesn't let water in.

All-rubber boots may be best for extended wet-weather hunting. In snake country, many hunters appreciate the protection of calf-high, leather snake boots.

Rubber soles with a shallow tread are best for turkey hunting in flat to rolling terrain. They are quiet, do not hold mud, and provide sufficient traction. Lug-soled boots are noisy and pick up lots of mud, but may be necessary in steep, rocky turkey habitat. Since the boot soles of a sitting hunter are likely to be facing the turkey as it approaches, dark or camouflage soles are better than light-colored ones.

Blisters or sore feet can ruin a turkey hunt, so break in new boots before the hunting season. Keep them serviceable and waterproof by following the manufacturer's use-and-care recommendations. When traveling to hunt turkeys, always pack two pairs of boots – one insulated and the other non-insulated. And tuck an extra pair of bootlaces into a pocket of your turkey vest.

SOCKS. Two pairs of socks are usually more comfortable than a single pair. A thin, polypropylene inner sock protects against blisters and wicks moisture away from skin. Outer socks should be either all wool or a wool-polypropylene blend. Lightweight wool is sufficient in warm weather; heavy wool insulates in cold weather. Cotton tends to hold moisture. For a refreshing break, carry an extra pair of socks in your vest or fanny pack, and change at midday.

PANTS. Two types of pants will cover nearly all conditions turkey hunters encounter. Lightweight cotton is perfect for warm, dry weather. Heavier, brushed cotton provides a bit more insulation for cooler days. During the rare cold snap, long underwear under the heavier pants will suffice. In the mountainous West, wool or fleece may be necessary during early seasons when cold rain or snow is likely.

Pants should have a soft finish that doesn't rasp noisily against brush and weeds. Deep pockets keep contents from spilling out when you sit against a tree. Cargo pockets are handy for carrying extra gear. Draw-strings at the cuffs protect against ticks and help keep pants cuffs dry in wet weather. Inseams should be long enough to prevent trouser cuffs from pulling up over boot tops when you sit on the ground with knees up, exposing skin, long underwear or light-colored socks.

SHIRTS. Shirts should cover your arms, but if it's too hot for long sleeves, combine a camouflage T-shirt with a mesh jacket or cover exposed skin with camouflage make-up. Worsterlon® is an effective synthetic in cool, wet weather. It performs like wool without the itch. For additional insulation, carry a camouflage sweater with Windstopper® lining.

COATS. A turkey hunter's coat should be uninsulated, camouflaged, and soft-finished to slip quietly through brush. It should be long enough so it won't ride up your back when you sit against a tree. Because you'll likely wear a coat for only a few hours in the morning, choose one that can be easily stuffed into a fanny pack or vest pocket. Often you can do without the coat altogether, especially if you already have a Windstopper sweater and Gore-Tex rainwear.

RAINGEAR. Rain is common during spring seasons, so savvy hunters prepare for it. A good choice is a lightweight, uninsulated camouflage pants-and-jacket rain suit made from a waterproof, breathable material such as Gore-Tex. Leg zippers allow you to easily slip pants on and off over boots. Since hoods block peripheral vision and hearing, a waterproof hat is preferable.

GLOVES. Because a turkey hunter's hands are frequently in motion – working a call or shifting a shotgun into position – disguising them with camouflage gloves is important. Gloves for turkey hunting should be lightweight so you can easily manipulate calls as well as the shotgun safety and trigger. If your gloves don't have a slit in the trigger finger (below),

you can cut the trigger finger of the glove off. Gloves with long cuffs can be pulled up over your shirt sleeves to ensure that no skin is exposed and to protect against ticks and insects.

FACE COVERS. A head net (right), face mask, or face paint will conceal the skin on your face which often "shines" in the sunlight. Each can be worn with or without a hat and are a must when hunting turkeys. Lightweight mesh materials or face paint are preferred in hot weather.

Effect of UV Brighteners on Turkeys

A WILD TURKEY is capable of seeing the ultraviolet end of the light spectrum, which is invisible to the human eye. For this reason, it is important that hunters do not contaminate their clothing with ultraviolet brighteners. UV brighteners are commonly found in most laundry detergents. When you wash hunting clothes in these detergents, they appear brighter to turkeys. Although turkeys are accustomed to seeing ultraviolet objects, such as flowers and rotting logs, these objects are stationary and do not startle turkeys. But a hunter moving through woods or simply moving an arm to raise his gun is more likely to be spotted if his clothing glows with ultraviolet brighteners. A simple solution is to treat camouflage clothes with UV KILLER, a product that blocks ultraviolet light. Always wash hunting clothing in a detergent such as Sport-Wash®, which does not contain UV brighteners. Much camouflage clothing today is manufactured without UV brighteners. To test clothing for UV brightener contamination, hold the material under a black light. It will glow if contaminated.

Accessories

Turkey hunters are fond of gadgets and gizmos. Hunters new to the sport often take to the woods loaded down with unnecessary equipment. As a hunter gains experience, though, he learns that too much gear is a hindrance to effective hunting. Stealth is the name of the turkey-hunting game, and it's hard to slip quietly through timber when overburdened with equipment. A veteran turkey hunter may own a ton of gear, but for any given hunt he leaves most of it behind, selecting only those items likely to be useful on that particular day.

Perhaps the most essential accessory is a lightweight camouflage vest with specialty pouches and pockets designed to store calls and other accessories within easy reach. Proper fit is critical. Your vest should be large enough to fit comfortably over a jacket. Better vests have a flip-down foam seat cushion, a foam insert that cushions your back when sitting against a tree, and a blaze-orange back flap that can be exposed for safety when carrying a gobbler from the woods. Some hunters opt for an inexpensive camouflage waist pack instead of a vest.

Other accessories commonly used by turkey hunters include: toilet paper, change of socks, orange game sack for carrying out turkey, water jug, maps, small camera, compact binoculars, compass, matches in waterproof case, small pruning shears, small knife, rain gear, candy bars, plastic bags for protecting gear from rain or for carrying internal organs after field-dressing a turkey, insect repellent, sunscreen, first-aid kit with moleskin for blisters and flashlight.

TURKEY VESTS are popular with most turkey hunters. The best vests have: (1) adjustable shoulder straps, (2) large front storage pockets, (3) a game pouch for carrying out your bird, (4) an orange safety flap and (5) an attached seat cushion.

CALLING
WILD TURKEY

Calling

Turkey calls have been an important part of the hunt ever since man discovered he could talk turkey and the birds would respond. Calls were made from a variety of materials, including turtle shells, coconuts, animal horns and bones, rocks and even old chewing tobacco containers. Some hand-made wooden box calls were so good they were passed down through many generations of turkey hunters.

Turkey calls have always been deadly at drawing toms to hunters. At one point in the early 1900s, calling for turkeys was considered so effective that some states made it illegal. Today, calling is not only legal, but considered by most devoted turkey hunters to be the only sporting way to take a gobbler.

Calling is the fun part of turkey hunting. Mastering a variety of different calls – learning when to yelp, cluck, purr or cutt, knowing when to call softly and when to crank up the volume – this is the art of spring turkey hunting. Don't short change yourself; learn to call well and you will enjoy the sport to its fullest. However, as important as calling is, woodsmanship is equally important. In fact, an accomplished woodsman – a hunter intimately familiar with the land and the turkeys that live on it – can take gobblers with amazing consistency without ever touching a call.

Under the right circumstances, turkeys can be ridiculously easy to call, even for beginners. But don't count on it. When hens are abundant or hunting pressure is heavy, only a hunter who has mastered the art of calling will walk out of the woods with a gobbler slung over a shoulder.

Calls designed to lure gobblers to the hunter can be divided into two broad categories: *friction calls* and *air-activated calls*. Although each has its advantages and disadvantages, the friction calls are generally easier to operate.

A third category of calls, *locator calls*, are used to elicit a response from a turkey without attracting the bird to your position. This response is most commonly referred to as a shock gobble. Turkeys have been known to *shock gobble* to the sound of a squeaking fence, slamming car door or a bellowing Holstein, and a host of other sudden, loud sounds. Most locator calls imitate animals such as crows, owls and coyotes, but loud cutting on a turkey call can also prompt a shock gobble.

There are dozens of commercial calls on the market, and while there is no need to buy and use all of them, a hunter is wise to use a variety of calls. Wild turkeys can be fickle, preferring a box call one morning, a diaphragm the next. A well-prepared hunter is ready to switch calls on those mornings when his old standbys just aren't making the grade.

Voice Calling

FEW MODERN HUNTERS ever master the art of voice calling turkeys the way 70-year-old Doyle Loadholtz has. "I started calling nearly 50 years ago, by whistling kee-kee calls," says Doyle. "But I didn't have much success making the other calls until a few years later. I caught a dandy cold during turkey season that year, and when the cold settled in my chest and throat, I found that I could bring the air up from way down in my gut through the chest cavity, regulating the amount escaping through the throat. That's the secret to mouth calling — regulating the air in your throat so you get that high-to-low pitch of a turkey."

"Don't worry about sounding like a turkey when you start out. Just work at making the sound descend from a high pitch down to a low pitch," advises Doyle. "It took me about 2 weeks to get the yelp down, but the first time I used it in the woods, I called in a gobbler. Then I went to work on the cluck. And once I had the cluck down, I learned how to gobble. The gobble is tough because it requires a rattle from deep in your throat at the same time you're making the sound. It's difficult to explain, but I'm convinced that anyone can learn to do it. Children pick up voice calling much quicker than adults. I suspect it has to do with the development of the vocal chords."

"Calling turkeys is fun no matter what call you use," says Doyle, who, after so many years, has not lost his enthusiasm for calling turkeys, although he rarely kills a gobbler anymore. "But there is something very special about calling one in using nothing but your voice. It also reduces the amount of equipment you have to carry into the woods; when you get to be my age, even a diaphragm call gets to be quite a load."

Friction Calls

Friction calls are easy to use, and, in the hands of a master, can realistically mimic the entire vocabulary of the wild turkey. Although the various friction calls are radically different in design, all operate on the same premise; one part rubs against the other to create sound.

BOX CALLS

The box call is the best known, easiest to use, and most popular of all friction calls. It is a favorite among beginners and experts alike.

Usually made of cedar or walnut, this device is a narrow, rectangular box with slightly arched sides that serve as sounding boards. The lid, or paddle, is attached to the back of the box with a hinge screw and extends to form a handle at the front. Scraping the round-bottomed paddle against the side lips of the box produces a variety of sounds, including yelps, clucks, cackles, cutts, purrs and even gobbles. Because a box call is loud, it is ideal on windy days or in heavy timber, where sound does not carry well.

Some box calls are tuned so the two sides produce different pitches. One side may imitate the raspy call of an old hen; the other, the higher-pitched sound of a younger bird.

Handle

Paddle, or lid

Lip

Side Panel

Sound Chamber

Hinge Screw

75

With proper care, a good box call will last decades. To prevent the wood from warping, keep the box dry. If you must use it on a rainy day, place it in a quart-size, resealable plastic bag. If it gets wet, dry it slowly at room temperature. When not using the box call, store it in a warm, dry location.

If oils from food, insect repellent or sunscreen contaminate the underside of the paddle or lips of the box, they can ruin the tone. To correct the problem, rub a non-oil-based chalk or carpenter's chalk on the underside of the paddle. If that does not solve the problem, sand the underside of the paddle lightly. Do not sand the lips of the box.

Every box call has a sweet spot, a point on the paddle that produces the perfect sound when scraped against the lip. Some calls are hand-tuned to the sweet spot by the manufacturer; others must be tuned by trial and error while you adjust the tension on the hinge screw at the back of the box. Once you have found the best tension, the paddle should scrape the lip at the exact same spot every time. Usually, the best sound is produced when the center of the paddle scrapes the lip.

HOW TO USE A BOX CALL

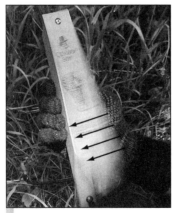 

YELP. Cradle the box call in your palm. Lightly scrape the paddle across the sounding board with 1-inch strokes. Do not lift, pop or put pressure on the paddle. The yelp is one note repeated 3 to 7 times.

CLUCK. A short, ¼-inch upward stroke of the paddle along the lip produces this call. Try to "pop" the paddle off the lip of the sounding board. Clucks can be used alone or to begin or end a series of yelps.

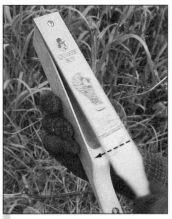

CUTT. This is a series of 10 to 15 sharp, rapidly repeated clucks. Cutting is mainly used to locate gobblers, not call them in, but can be used as a last resort to convince a reluctant gobbler to move into range.

PURR. This call is made by slowly and lightly dragging the paddle across the lip for 1 to 1 1/2 inches. The purr is used in conjunction with soft clucking.

CACKLE. Begin with a couple of yelps, then sharply strike the paddle against the lip in short, 1/2-inch strokes a half-dozen times. Trail off with 2 or 3 yelps.

GOBBLE. Slip a #12 rubber band around the body of the call near the handle. Hold the call handle-end-up, and shake it vigorously side to side. Do not use if other hunters are nearby.

SCRATCH BOX

A scratch box looks like a small box call without the hinged paddle. Although its sound chamber is smaller, it makes a high-pitched sound that carries a considerable distance. The scratch box is best suited for mimicking yelps, clucks and purrs, but in the hands of an experienced caller, it can imitate all hen turkey calls.

YELPS. Drag the striker across the lip of the box. Change pitch by increasing or decreasing the angle of the striker. Some scratch boxes are tuned so each lip produces a different tone.

CLUCKS. Create these short, choppy sounds with a short stroke of the striker, then pop it off the lip.

PURRS. Scrape the striker slowly across the lip of the box with moderate pressure.

A scratch box requires little care. Chalk the underside of the striker periodically, and if the lip of the box becomes dirty, lightly sand it with fine sandpaper.

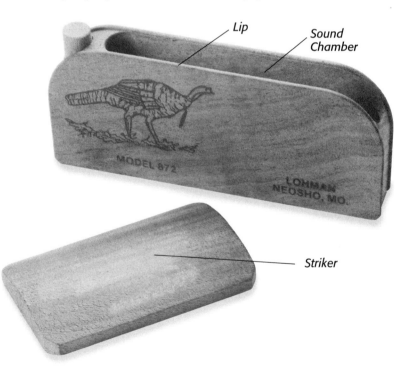

Lip

Sound Chamber

Striker

PUSH-PULL CALLS

The easiest of all calls to master, push-pull calls are sometimes called "idiot boxes" because they are so easy to operate. Some hunters refuse to use this call because of its reputation as a foolproof aid for amateurs, but in reality the push-pull call should be a part of every hunter's arsenal, beginner and expert alike. Its only drawbacks: It requires some hand motion to operate, and it won't work when wet.

QUICK TIP:
Create a "talking" decoy by securing a push-pull call to the decoy stake. Tie a long string to the plunger so you can operate the call from your position.

Correctly tuned, a push-pull call is one of the most realistic you can use. A wire tension spring (below) or rubber band controls the plunger

Striking Surface

Striker

Tension Spring

Plunger

tension. By adjusting this tension, you can change the pitch of the call. When the tone changes or the call begins to squeak, rub chalk on the striking surface.

A push-pull call is best suited for yelping, purring and clucking. Experienced callers can also make it cutt. Different sounds are produced by changing the speed, cadence and length of the plunger strokes.

QUICK TIP:
Use a push-pull call designed to attach to the barrel of a gun. The call is secured with a Velcro® strap and has a string attached to the plunger.

Using the "Fighting Purr"

THE FIGHTING PURR is a variation of the push-pull call. It can be either a single call with dual push rods or two separate calls, tuned to different pitches.

As David Hale, an early developer of the fighting purr call, observes, "Aggressive purring creates a sudden sense of urgency in a gobbler. I've seen how toms react when watching two other birds fighting. Their heads change in color from white to blood red as they become increasingly agitated, and after watching a battle, these toms are ready for war.

"The goal of the fighting purr call is to create the sounds of such a fight. In the right situation, it is one of the most effective calls I know for bringing in gobblers."

Why are gobblers drawn so irresistibly to the sounds of two other toms in combat? It may be because they sense an opportunity to move up in the flock hierarchy should a dominant tom be defeated. Or perhaps they are lured in hopes of courting a hen while the toms are preoccupied.

HOW TO USE A PUSH-PULL CALL (Shown cut-away for clarity)

YELP. Hold the box lightly in one hand. With your index finger, push the plunger in a series of 3 to 7 smooth 1/2-inch strokes. Some hunters prefer to pull the plunger.

PURR. Push or pull the plunger slowly and steadily in 1/2-inch strokes, causing the striker to skip across the surface of the peg and create a staccato vibration.

CLUCK. Tap the plunger sharply with the palm of your hand, end of your index finger or against your leg. Because the cluck is an abrupt call, the plunger moves only 1/4 inch.

SLATE-AND-PEG CALLS

The slate-and-peg call probably originated when some primitive hunter picked up a piece of flat slate, rubbed a stick against it and noticed that it sounded like a turkey.

Over the years, hunters and call manufacturers have tried various substitutes for slate, including glass and aluminum. Regardless of the striking surface, this type of device is most commonly known as a slate-and-peg call. Using a slate-and-peg requires practice, but the skill is not difficult to master. This call is a favorite with traditionalists who prefer time-honored methods. Expert callers like the slate-and-peg for its versatility. Just by varying the stroke pattern and peg pressure, a good caller can simulate any call of the hen turkey.

SLATE & PEG CALLS come in many styles, but all use a similar design. A hollow wood or plastic pot (1), usually with holes drilled in the bottom to provide resonance, holds the striking surface (2). A wood or plastic peg (3) is rubbed across the striking surface to create sound. Hold the pot so that your thumb and middle finger are opposite each other. The pot should be held loosely so it can swivel between these two pressure points. Hold the peg like a pencil, thumb in center of peg. The peg should lie ¼ inch behind the knuckle on the index finger, and rest midway between the last joint and the tip of the middle finger. Only about ½ to 1 inch of the peg should extend past the tip of the middle finger. The volume and pitch of the call is controlled by increasing or decreasing pressure on the peg.

All slate-and-peg calls have a "sweet spot" – a small spot on the striking surface that produces the most realistic sound. Once you find this spot, file a notch in the pot's rim so you can locate the sweet spot even in the dark.

A peg makes no noise when rubbed on a smooth surface, so the slate must be roughed up with a piece of Scotch-Brite™. Four to six strokes in one direction are plenty. This process, called "dressing," should be done any time the slate becomes smooth or difficult to make a sound on. For a glass surface, use 80-grit silicone-carbide sandpaper, commonly called drywall paper. Then use a clean cotton cloth to wipe away dust. Do not wipe with your hand or blow the dust off, or you may put body oil or moisture on the surface. If the tip of the peg is dirty or oily, clean it by scraping it (not sharpening it) with the blade of a pocket knife, or sanding with 220-grit paper.

Protect your call by carrying it in a resealable plastic bag or plastic container. Calls with wooden pots are especially sensitive to moisture. If they do get wet, allow them to dry slowly. Never lay calls on the dashboard of your vehicle, or anyplace else where they will be subjected to intense heat. During the off season, store them in a dry area where temperatures are stable.

HOW TO USE A SLATE-AND-PEG CALL

All of the different calls made with a slate-and-peg require that the peg remain in contact with the striking surface at all times.

(1) YELP. Scribe a football-shaped pattern about the size of a dime on the striking surface, using the tip of the peg.

(2) PURR. Move your thumb slightly higher on the rod, apply moderate pressure and slowly drag the peg toward yourself. The peg should skip lightly across the surface of the slate.

(3) CLUCK. Apply extra pressure to the peg with an index finger; push down and pull the peg toward yourself. It should jump sharply, but not leave the slate surface.

(4) CUTT. Use the cluck stroke, but continue slightly longer and repeat rapidly 6 to 8 times.

Air-Activated Calls

DIAPHRAGM CALLS are available in numerous reed configurations, including (1) single reed, (2) double reed, (3) triple reed and (4) stacked reed. Split or notched reeds (5) are common.

Air-activated calls include diaphragm calls, tube calls and wingbone calls. Although these differ greatly from one another, all produce sound from air vibrations.

DIAPHRAGM CALLS

The diaphragm, generally regarded as the most versatile of all turkey calls, consists of one or more thin layers of latex rubber stretched across a horseshoe-shaped frame in the center of a plastic skirt. Because the device fits inside the mouth, it requires no hand movement to operate, a big advantage when dealing with a bird adept at detecting the slightest movement. The diaphragm call is inexpensive and small enough that a half dozen can easily be carried in a small pouch.

The only drawback to the diaphragm call is that it can be difficult to master. Producing the first sound without gag-

ging can be quite a chal-
lenge. But most hunters
find that once they are able
to make a noise – any noise
– learning to produce
turkey talk comes quickly.
The best way to master the
diaphragm call is to practice
while listening to a good
tape. Start with a single-reed
call, because it is the easiest
to blow.

> QUICK TIP:
> Avoid "latex mouth,"
> the sour taste of a
> diaphragm call in
> your mouth for long
> periods, by pouring
> a few drops of
> mouthwash in your
> call container.

To prevent latex diaphragms from sticking to one another,
rinse in water, allow to dry (not in the sun) and store in
individual containers or separated by pieces of wax paper.
A flat toothpick between the reeds of multiple-reed models
prevents sticking. Store in the refrigerator.

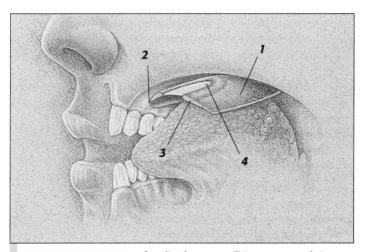

PROPER PLACEMENT of a diaphragm call in your mouth is crucial to success. (1) Use your tongue to position the call against
the roof of your mouth with the straight edge facing forward.
(2) Position the call so the forward edge nearly touches the
back of your top front teeth. (3) Place the top of your tongue
lightly against the latex reed, (4) expel short bursts of air
between the top of your tongue and the reed, while saying the
word "chirp." Stay at it, and you will soon be able to produce
acceptable yelps, the first call you should learn. Once you have
mastered the yelp, begin practicing other calls.

TUBE CALLS

Tube calls, early models of which were made from snuffboxes, produce sounds unlike that of other turkey calls. This feature makes the tube call a good choice on hard-hunted property where gobblers have heard it all before. The tube call is nothing more than a hollow plastic tube with a reed of latex rubber stretched over one end.

The tube call works best for producing excited, high-pitched yelping and cutting with maximum volume, although a master caller can also make soft, mellow

TUBE CALLS usually consist of an open-ended cylinder made from molded plastic, with a strip of latex stretched over one end and held in place with a rubber band. Different styles of tube calls include: (1) molded plastic commercial tube, (2) homemade, from a 35mm film canister and (3) a modern version of the old snuffbox.

yelps and clucks. Because of its volume and unique pitch, many top-notch hunters consider the tube call to be an ideal locator for inciting a gobble from a reluctant tom.

To use the tube call, position your bottom lip against the latex, and cup your hands around the opposite end of the call. Expel air through the call so the latex vibrates.

Tuning a tube call is accomplished by adjusting the gap between the latex and the edge of the call. Always make sure that the latex is taut. Hunters who rely heavily upon the tube call often carry a spare strip of latex and a couple of rubber bands in case a rubber band breaks or the latex needs replacing.

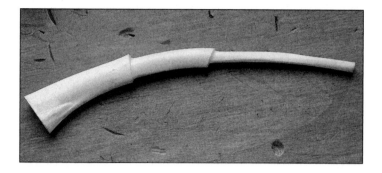

WINGBONE CALLS

There is something special about calling in a gobbler using a call you have made from the bones of the species you hunt. The design for this call originated in the southern United States nearly 200 years ago, and there are still a few old-time craftsmen who make and sell wingbones by special order. Manufactured wingbone yelpers made from plastic and wood are also available, but most hunters derive more enjoyment from making their own.

The traditional wingbone yelper is usually formed from two or three hen turkey wing bones. Some hunters prefer the lower-pitched tone produced by jake or tom wing bones. Domestic turkeys' wing bones are too thin, porous and fragile. Wingbone yelpers are not easy to master, but with a lot of practice you can learn to produce excellent yelps and clucks. Because the sound of each wingbone call is unique, they are effective on hard-hunted gobblers. Hunters who become proficient on the wingbone call usually prefer it over all others.

To use a wingbone call, put the flat, smaller end between your lips, near the corner of your mouth, and grip your hands around the end of the call. Suck sharply on the call with a kissing motion so your lips vibrate on the mouthpiece. Practice until you can make a sound resembling a turkey.

HOW TO MAKE A WINGBONE CALL

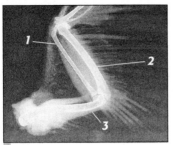

BONES needed to make a wingbone yelper are the radius (1) and ulna (2). The humerus (3) can also be used if you want a 3-bone yelper.

REMOVE these bones from the wing with a sharp knife. Cut away as much meat and gristle as you can. Separate from one another.

CUT both ends of bones with a fine-toothed saw. Remove marrow by running a wire through the bones while holding under running water.

BOIL bones in warm, soapy water for an hour, then give them a final rinsing. To whiten them, soak in a solution of hydrogen peroxide.

BEVEL the cut edges of the bones with fine-grit sandpaper until smooth. You may need to recut and resand the ends to fit the bones properly.

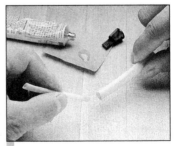

PLACE the round end of the radius bone into the small end of the ulna bone, until they fit snugly. Secure the joint with epoxy.

Locator calls

Locator calls are designed to shock a tom into gobbling to reveal its position. Turkeys often respond to any loud, sudden noise, but the safest locator calls mimic natural sounds, such as owls, crows, coyotes, hawks, pileated woodpeckers and even bull elk. Turkey calls can also be used to locate gobblers. Loud, excited yelps and cutts are most effective.

Most mornings, gobblers sound off on their own, but if you have not heard a gobble by the time it is light enough to distinguish individual trees, blow an owl hooter to elicit a gobble. If that fails, try other non-turkey locator calls.

Keep your first locator call short, or you'll drown out any reply. For instance, instead of the traditional "who-cooks-for-you, who-cooks-for-you-all" rendition of the barred owl, just give one short, loud squall on an owl hooter. Then listen. Same for a crow call. Two or three short, chopped-off calls, sounding like "caw-caw-caw," afford you a much better chance to hear any gobbler that responds to your call.

DEPENDABLE LOCATOR CALLS include: (1) owl hooter, (2) coyote howler with large bellows, (3) flute-style goose call, (4) silent whistle with adjustable frequency, (5) crow call, (6) pileated woodpecker call, (7) hawk screamer and (8) predator call.

Many hunters believe it is best to use non-turkey sounds prior to the morning fly-down, and then to use turkey calls after the birds are on the ground. Some experts believe it is always best to try to elicit a gobble with a non-turkey call first, no matter the circumstances. A hunter who begins with yelps and cutts runs the risk of being surprised by a quiet tom that sneaks in unannounced. A non-turkey call surprises a tom into announcing his location, but does not lure him closer. The hunter has plenty of time to set up before making hen calls.

While listening for gobbles is the most important consideration when using a locator call, don't tune out other sounds. If you hear hens yelping, odds are there is a gobbler nearby. Also listen for other hunters. Most give their locations away by overcalling. Knowing the whereabouts of other hunters can help you devise a hunting plan that ensures that you are not hunting the same bird.

Anyone can hear a turkey gobble 200 yards away on a calm morning, but it requires concentration to hear a bird a half mile away, or one tucked down in a valley when the wind is blowing. Under these conditions, you won't hear the entire gobble, but listen intently and you'll hear enough, usually the last "gobble," to get a fix on his position. When listening for a gobble, stand still, with your mouth open, and move only your head; shifting your body rustles clothing. Don't unwrap a candy bar, shuffle your feet or light a cigarette. If hunting with a partner, stand at least 30 feet apart so that you are not talking when you should be listening.

Don't give up on your prime location too soon. If your scouting has convinced you there are gobblers in the area, then this is where you want to spend that magical half-hour prior to sunrise. And don't go charging off as soon as you hear that first gobble, because gobbles often have a ventriloquistic quality to them, which makes it difficult to pinpoint their exact location. Stay put and listen for more gobbling, going to the bird only when you are certain of its location.

Getting a bird to shock gobble simply means you scared or surprised it. The response was strictly reflex. If you cannot coax subsequent gobbles from the bird, the odds of killing him are slim. Rather than attempt to hunt such a reluctant tom, search for another. But remember the location of every gobble you hear. Return in an hour or so, and that same gobbler may be anxious to answer your calls. Walking away from a gobbler is tough but is often the smartest move when a bird gobbles only once.

The easiest way to learn to use locator calls is by practicing with an instructional tape. Many manufacturers of locator calls package their products with such tapes.

Locating Longbeards

I was hunting the coulee country of southeastern Minnesota, not far from the mighty Mississippi River. The evening before, I had watched five toms scratch for newly planted corn, then walk up a shallow timbered valley to roost. There was confidence in every step I took the next morning as I hiked up the valley where the gobblers had roosted. It's not every morning you know where there is one gobbler, let alone five.

Whenever possible, I like to let gobblers crank up on their own. That way I don't worry about giving away my location. By the time the cardinals and chickadees were in full voice, the fivesome had not sounded off, so I gave them a hit from an owl hooter. Nothing. I tried again. Still no response. Then I tried a coyote howler. Same results. It grew lighter. I hit them hard with my crow call. Silence. I was dumfounded.

Unless something had spooked the birds off the roost during the night, they had to be here. As I pondered my next move, I heard the distant rumble of a barge pushing its load up the river. The captain must have cranked up the engines to negotiate his cargo around a corner, and when he did, the big diesel responded with a steady "whump, whump, whump." Those gobblers, which turned out to be roosted only 70 yards from where I stood, went nuts, every one of them trying to outgobble the other. That's when I hit my slate call and sent out a sleepy series of yelps. Those longbeards flew down and all but tripped over each other racing to the sound of my call. I took the biggest one, and the rest just stood there gobbling at the sound of my shot. You just never know what's going to trip a gobbler's trigger.

Gary Clancy

PREPARING
FOR THE HUNT

Gathering Information

Preparation for a wild turkey hunt begins months before you actually don camouflage and head for the woods. The more information you gather prior to the season, the better your chances for a successful hunt.

Your best source of information is a turkey biologist in the state you plan to hunt. Call that state's wildlife agency and request the phone number of a turkey biologist. He or she can tell you which areas have the highest turkey populations, where there are large areas of public land, and at what time during the season you can expect the most gobbling.

This information will get you started, but savvy hunters dig deeper. Try to find areas where wild turkeys have been recently introduced, and check to see if hunting seasons are held there. Hunting pressure will be light in these new regions compared to the more popular areas where there is a tradition of turkey hunting.

When looking for public lands, most hunters turn to wildlife management areas or national forest land, sometimes overlooking other possibilities, including state forest lands, national wildlife refuges, corporate timber holdings, and corps of engineers property, especially around reservoirs.

Talk to the people who spend much of their time in turkey country: farmers, loggers, surveyors, linemen, rural mailmen, milk haulers, school bus drivers, and county employees who operate road graders and snow plows. Bring a thermos of hot coffee and strike up a conversation. These folks are often eager to take a break and talk about local wildlife.

If you plan to hunt out-of-state, start the ball rolling early. In states that hold drawings to assign turkey licenses, your application may be due before the first of the year. Familiarize yourself with all regulations for the state you plan to hunt, since they may differ from those in your home state. Some states, for instance, do not allow the use of decoys. Others require proof of having completed a firearms safety or hunter education course before you can obtain a nonresident hunting license. If you haven't completed such a course, obtaining a certificate could take several months.

MAPS. Unless you hunt a small parcel you know as intimately as the inside of your garage, maps will be essential to a productive hunt. Maps of state and national forests, wildlife management areas, national refuges and corps of engineers lands are available from government agencies.

Timber companies usually sell maps of their holdings at nominal cost. These will help you navigate timber company lands and ensure that you don't wander onto adjacent private property.

County highway maps, usually for sale at county courthouses or highway department offices, show all state, county and township roads, and are invaluable for keeping your bearings in a new region.

If you plan to hunt on private land, buy a plat book, also available at the county courthouse, which lists landowners and shows property boundaries. When seeking permission to hunt private land, ask the owner to outline property boundaries on your plat book map.

U.S. Geological Survey (USGS) topographic maps, often called "topo" maps, are available from USGS offices or local map stores. These include contour lines depicting hills, valleys and ridges – information a turkey hunter needs. They also show roads, trails, buildings, fields, clearcuts, streams, rivers, lakes and timber stands. A topo map with a 1:2400 scale covers about 50 square miles, more country than a turkey hunter can cover. When you have chosen precise hunting areas, copy and enlarge only those squares of the map.

Aerial photos cover 1 square mile each and provide detail not found on topo maps. Unfortunately, aerial photos are not available for every section in every county. Check with the Agricultural Stabilization and Conservation Service (ASCS) in the county you plan to hunt, for aerial photos.

Aerial photos can be ordered from:
Aerial Photography Field Office,
User Services
P.O. Box 30010
Salt Lake City, UT 84130
Phone (801) 975-3503

Topographical maps can be ordered from:
USGS Information Services
P.O. Box 25286
Denver, CO 80225
Phone 1-800-USA-MAPS

Scouting

For an experienced hunter, the turkey-hunting ritual begins well before the season opens. His goal is to locate 10 to 12 areas that hold gobblers. This kind of painstaking scouting will give you a big edge over hunters who simply arrive in the woods on opening day. First, you'll be hunting with anticipation and excitement, confident there are turkeys in the area. Second, knowing the stomping grounds of a dozen gobblers gives you options on mornings when your bird of choice is not gobbling, or when another hunter has encroached on your turf. A less

DRIVE to as many good listening points as possible. Call only if birds are not gobbling on their own.

prepared hunter without any preseason scouting under his belt is out of luck if he hears no gobbling on opening day.

Whether you hunt public land or private, having access to as much territory as possible is critical to success. For example, if you discover a farm bursting with wild turkeys, get permission to hunt it – but try to get permission to hunt surrounding farms as well. Few things are more frustrating than watching gobblers strutting just over the fence on land you cannot hunt.

Begin scouting about one month before the season begins – the time when wild turkeys begin gobbling. Spend early morning scouting sessions listening for gobbles from high areas where you can hear well. Carry a map, and mark spots where you hear gobbles. On a good morning it's possible to drive to a half-dozen good listening areas before gobbling subsides.

When toms fall quiet at midmorning, seek high vantage points to glass fields and pastures where turkeys spend much of their time. Good binoculars will help you locate birds, but it often takes a spotting scope to distinguish toms from hens.

Once you identify a good hunting area by hearing or seeing turkeys, hike the terrain before the season opens, especially if you'll be hunting it for the first time. Your goal now is not to locate turkeys, but to learn the lay of the land. Don't do any calling while scouting or you'll make gobblers call-wise. Don't worry about disturbing turkeys during a scouting mission. Wild turkeys have short memories, and within an hour of being rousted they return to normal behavior.

TYPES OF TURKEY SIGN

DROPPINGS from toms (left) resemble cigarette butts, often with a J-shaped hook at the end. Hen droppings (inset) usually have no definable form. Each turkey leaves at least two dozen droppings a day.

SCRATCHINGS are found where turkeys have scraped the ground while feeding on nuts, seeds and insects. Fresh scratchings are moist; old scratchings are dried out.

Pay attention to fields and pastures where turkeys feed and strut, and look for creeks, ravines and other barriers that may prevent a gobbler from moving from those fields to your calls. While hiking the area, keep an eye peeled for turkey sign. Droppings, tracks, scratchings, dusting areas and drag marks can tell you much about turkey activity in the area.

Although gobblers are not as vocal in the evening, a loud locator call can induce them to gobble from the roost. Coyote howlers, owl hooters and predator calls are especially effective. If you are scouting a large area, drive from one good listening area to another and call several times from each location. If your hunting area is limited, hike the high ground and howl or hoot from all good listening points. Gobblers are most responsive from one hour prior to sundown until dark.

DUSTING AREAS are likely in dry dirt or fine sand, including old roadbeds, field edges and dry streambeds. Such areas are marked by shallow depressions where the birds have dusted.

TRACKS can identify sex. An adult tom's middle toe is generally more than 2½ inches long. Jake and hen middle toes are less than 2½ inches. Turkeys walk about 4 miles a day.

SCOUTING TIPS

SEARCH forested habitat for roosting sites. Birds living in wooded areas rarely roost in the same tree two nights in a row. Prairie and brush country birds, however, often use the same tree for generations. Identify popular roost sites by the abundance of droppings present.

LOCATE traditional spring strutting zones. When scouting familiar ground, always return to places where you have heard gobblers in the past. If one is killed, another often takes over his territory.

LOOK for flocks in fall and winter. Adult toms usually form small bachelor groups apart from small hen flocks. These disperse before spring. Where you find turkeys in the fall, you'll probably find them in spring.

MANY TURKEY HUNTERS consider calling the most important aspect of the hunt, taking basic woodsman-ship for granted. In reality, knowing your way around the woods often is the most important factor dictating success. A map and compass is consiered essential by tradition-alists, but more and more modern hunters are turning to a high-tech, electronic device — the GPS (Global Positioning System). Used correctly, a hand-held GPS is easier to use and more versatile than a com-pass and map.

Using a GPS for Turkey Hunting

The GPS is a battery-operated electronic receiver that tracks signals from three satellites in stationary orbit above the earth. A small, specialized com-puter in the GPS uses these satellite signals to triangulate your position. The GPS can also store and recall these coordi-nates, and can guide you back to any position, or "waypoint," that has been saved in the computer's memory.

A GPS is particularly helpful when you're hunting a large, unfamiliar tract of land. During your scouting expeditions, use the GPS to record the coordi-nates for promising hunting spots and known roosting trees. Also record the coordinates for your base camp. Some GPS devices can store hundreds of such way-points. In the predawn hours on hunting day, call up the desired waypoint on the GPS, and follow the recommended heading shown on the screen. A GPS has several different screen modes, but the easiest to use is the mode that shows "bearing-to-waypoint" and "distance-to-go" (DTG) readouts. Simply walk in the compass direction shown on the screen, stopping periodically to recalculate the heading. If you've strayed off route, the GPS will compensate and recommend a new head-ing. A built-in alarm beeps soft-ly as you near your destination. At the end of a long day of hunting, you can call up your base camp coordinates to find your way home.

GPS devices work best in open areas with a clear, wide view of the sky. They are only accurate to within about 50 yards, so don't expect a GPS to guide you to a single bush in a dense forest. And carry a map and old-fashioned compass as a backup. As with any electronic device, a GPS can break down or lose power. Carrying extra batteries is always a good idea.

Understanding Daily Patterns

To effectively hunt wild turkeys in spring, a hunter must understand the bird's daily movement patterns. Bagging a wild turkey is largely a matter of being in the right place at the right time.

At first light, as turkeys begin to awaken in their roosting trees, toms begin to gobble, while hens utter soft tree yelps. Usually the birds fly to the ground as soon as there is enough light for them to spot predators, but this fly-down can be as late as two hours after sunrise if the morning is rainy or foggy. Turkeys roosting in small wood lots in relatively open areas tend to fly down sooner than birds roosting in deep timber, where daylight is longer in arriving.

When a turkey gobbles on the roost in early morning, he is trying to draw a hen to him. If successful, the tom will fly down to join the hen. If a hen doesn't appear, the tom flies down and walks to his strutting area, while continuing to gobble.

Strutting zones are located in open areas where toms can be easily seen by hens, such as a field edge, logging road or pasture. In hill country, strutting areas are often located on elevated ridges, points or hilltops. In flat country, gobblers often strut in semi-open hardwood bottoms.

When the tom arrives at the strutting zone, he continues to gobble until he attracts a hen. Once a hen arrives, however, the gobbler begins to strut and his gobbling becomes infrequent. The tom may attract several hens simultaneously.

A gobbler follows hens as they wander to feed, mating with each several times during the morning, if they permit. Identifying feeding areas can be difficult, since wild turkeys eat such a wide variety of food. In big timber,

turkeys often wander along, foraging on whatever they find. In agricultural areas, turkeys feed in crop fields a good deal of the time.

Only in the arid regions of the West and Southwest do turkeys habitually seek water during their daily route. In most regions they obtain sufficient water from dew or in the plants they consume.

By mid- to late morning, after satisfying their hunger, turkeys often treat themselves to a dust bath. Bred hens may then retire to the nest to lay or incubate. Gobblers may rest at this time or resume gobbling and continue to search for new hens.

Midafternoon finds turkeys on the move and feeding once again. During the last hour of day, the flock feeds toward roosting sites. They usually fly up at sunset or shortly thereafter. Birds often change limbs or even roosting trees a number of times before settling in for the night.

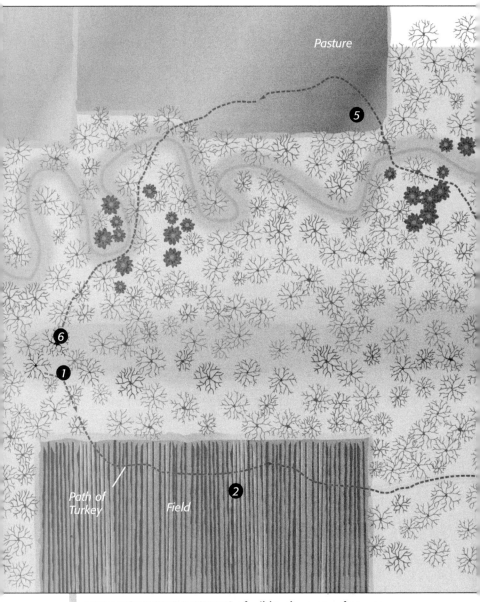

DAILY MOVEMENT PATTERNS of wild turkeys are often pre-dictable. (1) At first light, toms begin to gobble on the roost. When it is light enough to see the ground, toms fly down. If gobbling from the roost has not attracted hens, toms continue to gobble while walking to their strutting zones, where they display to draw hens. (2) After attracting one or more hens, the

104

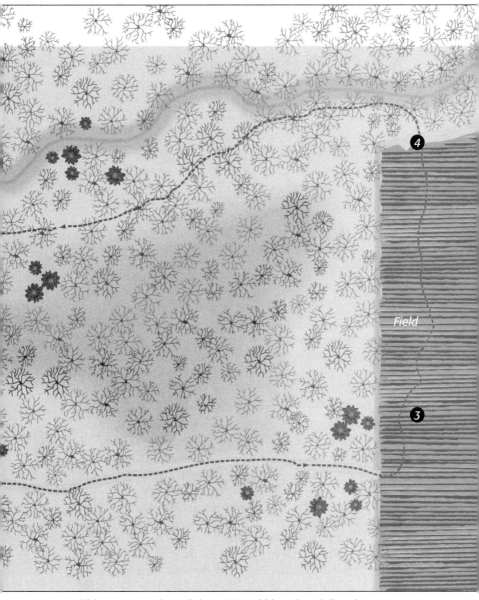

Field

gobbler mates with each hen. (3) Gobblers then follow hens to feeding areas, often in fields. (4) At some point during the day, turkeys usually take a dust bath. When hens retire to their nests, toms may wander in search of other hens. (5) In late afternoon, birds feed again as they move toward roosting trees, where they (6) fly up to roost at dusk.

Patterning Shotguns

A turkey can be cleanly killed only when hit solidly in the skull and neck vertebrae – a target considerably smaller than your hand and forearm. Body shots often cripple because heavy breast muscles and nearly impenetrable wing feathers shield a wild turkey's vital internal organs. A ballistics study by Winchester/Olin found that a minimum of three pellets must fully penetrate the bird's brain or neck vertebrae to ensure a clean kill.

When patterning your shotgun, use a life-size target of a turkey's head and neck showing shaded vital areas. Stake this target 3 feet off the ground 25 yards from a tree. Sit against the tree and shoot your shotgun just as you would in an actual hunting situation. Since similar loads can show marked differences in pattern, depending on manufacturer, it is best to shoot as many brands of No. 4, 5 and 6 shot as possible. Buffered loads of copper or nickel-plated shot pattern best. Use the choke you plan to hunt with – preferably a full, extra-full, or tight custom choke. Repeat the procedure at 30, 35 and 40 yards – the recommended maximum shooting range.

After each shot, record the load, choke and gun used, and range on the target. At the end of the session, you'll be able to count vital hits and easily determine which load patterns best in your shotgun.

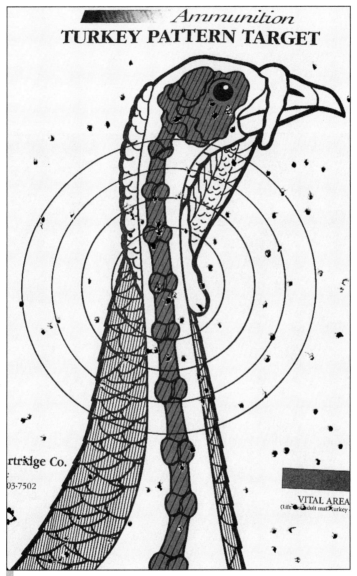

Ammunition
TURKEY PATTERN TARGET

rtridge Co.

03-7502

VITAL AREA
(Life size adult male turkey)

KILLING SHOTS require at least 3 pellets in the vital (brain and neck vertebrae) zone of the head and neck. This pattern with a dozen vital hits is the kind of performance you are looking for.

TURKEY HUNTING
TECHNIQUES

Basic Hunting Techniques

With its sharp eyesight, acute hearing and naturally wary, nervous manner, hunting the wild turkey is a challenge. But learning to successfully hunt this bird is not as difficult as it first appears. Turkeys are susceptible to good calling, respond readily to decoys and have predictable daily habits. A well-equipped, disciplined hunter with a good understanding of wild turkey behavior has an excellent chance of shooting a tom.

The following pages describe typical turkey hunting tactics. Subsequent chapters describe adaptations for special situations.

LOCATING WILD TURKEYS

The first step in a successful hunt is to find good turkey habitat. Assuming you have scouted adequately, you should know several spots that hold birds.

Ideally, you'll want to "roost" a gobbler on the eve of the

SPOT A GOBBLER feeding or strutting in the open on the evening before your hunt, and you can bet the bird will not be far away in the morning. In typical farm country habitat, it is common to locate several birds in an evening.

hunt, which means you actually see or hear the bird in his roost tree. Return before first light, slip within 100 yards of this roost, sound a couple of tree yelps at dawn, and odds are good the gobbler will fly down practically in your lap.

To "put a bird to bed," set up near a roosting site in early evening. Turkeys feed toward a roost tree in late evening, usually fly into them around sunset, and settle in before dark. On a still evening, you can often hear their wings beating as they fly up. They make quite a racket while flapping from branch to branch, sometimes from tree to tree, before selecting the perfect bed. Hearing enhancers, such as the Walkers Game Ear®, help pinpoint these sounds.

If you cannot spot birds, listen for them. Occasionally, toms gobble a time or two after roosting, and hens sometimes yelp. More often, you'll have to make them gobble by using a locator call. Walk through likely habitat, pausing every quarter mile or so to call. If a gobbler responds, move toward him, eliciting additional shock gobbles until you've pinpointed his location. Mark the site and the trail to it with strips of toilet paper or surveyor's tape so you find your way back before dawn. On rare occasions, gobblers change roosts during the night, but in most cases they'll still be where you left them.

In agricultural areas, scan fields with binoculars in early evening. If you spot a gobbler feeding during the last minutes of day, you can be sure he won't be far away the next morning.

FIRST LIGHT

Whether or not you've roosted a tom the previous night, dawn is magical. At no other time will you hear so much gobbling. Your hunting tactic will vary, depending on whether you pinpointed a roosting tom.

If you did roost one, you'll have the luxury of sneaking to within 100 yards under cover of darkness. Turkeys like to fly down into open areas, so whenever possible, set up on the edge of a cleared area close to the roost tree. A hen decoy in the clearing can give you a big advantage.

As day breaks, give a few quiet tree yelps. Chances are good that the gobbler will reply, but if he doesn't, resist the temptation to call louder or more often. Overcalling while a tom is still on the roost is a common mistake.

If you're hunting hill country, remember that gobblers are much more likely to come to a call if you position yourself on the same level as the bird or slightly higher. Gobblers are reluctant to walk downhill to the call.

TYPICAL EARLY-MORNING SCENARIO

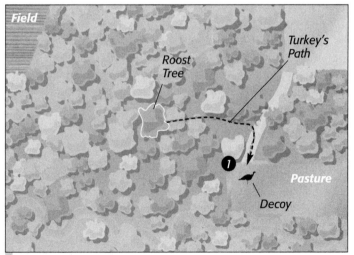

SET UP in the nearest opening to the roost tree, and put out a decoy (1). If the gobbler is alone, he will go to the field to gobble and strut. If he is with hens, he will tag along as they go to feed in the field. The logging road is the obvious approach route.

113

If you failed to put a gobbler to bed the night before, plan to be at a good listening position well before first light. Hilltops and ridges are best. On most mornings, toms begin gobbling spontaneously, but if you hear no gobbling by the time there is enough light for you to see individual limbs on trees, then try to elicit a gobble with an owl or crow call. When you hear a gobbler within reasonable distance, try to get within 100 yards before setting up to call him. If possible, set up along the edge of an open area and yelp softly a few times to begin.

Turkeys usually fly from the roost as soon as there is enough light for them to see predators on the ground. However, on rainy, foggy or unseasonably cold mornings, they may stay on the roost for an hour or more after sunrise. Nevertheless, if you haven't heard gobbling by the time it is fully light, assume the gobblers are already on the ground, heading for strutting areas or cavorting with hens.

Gobblers without hens are especially susceptible to excited yelping and clucking as they travel between the roost site and the strut zone.

They'll use the same strutting grounds day after day. These are usually in relatively open areas, such as open timber, field edges, pastures or logging roads, where toms can watch for approaching hens and hens can clearly see their strutting displays. Strutting grounds can be difficult to identify unless you actually see a bird strutting or find telltale wing-tip drag marks. But once you find these sites, you can hunt them productively for years, because turkeys return to the same strutting zones season after season. If one gobbler is killed, another moves in. Savvy hunters mark all strutting zones on a map.

Once at his "dance hall," a tom fans his tail, puffs his chest, drags his wing tips and walks proudly, pirouetting to display his finery. From time to time he sticks out his head and gobbles, adding an audio advertisement to his show. He may gobble enthusiastically to your hen yelps, but will probably not leave the strutting zone to come to your calls; hens are supposed to go to him, and he knows it. Hunters often make the mistake of yelping loudly and frequently in an effort to draw a tom closer, but this rarely works. It is better to play hard-to-get. Call just enough to let a gobbler know you are there. Every few minutes, scratch the ground to mimic the sound of a foraging turkey. This assures the gobbler that a hen is still nearby, but since she ignores his calling, he sometimes goes against his own instinct and sashays toward her.

Try to intercept and scare off any hens you see responding to the gobbler, even if it means risking being seen by the tom. The longer he struts without attracting a hen, the more likely he'll move your way. Once in female company, a gobbler will usually ignore you.

The prime early morning strutting/gobbling period may last a few minutes to an hour. Occasionally, a tom will return to his strutting zone in late morning after his original partners abandon him.

THE DEAD ZONE

After the excitement of the early morning gobbling period, the next two or three hours can be a letdown for hunters. Most mature gobblers are already with hens by this time and too busy strutting and breeding to gobble. Two strategies can produce results during this dead period: *run-and-gun,* or *sit-and-wait.*

In areas with good numbers of gobblers 3 years of age or older, younger toms do little breeding and are likely to respond to calls during the "dead period." To take advantage of them, use the run-and-gun approach; walk quickly through the area, stopping frequently to blow a locator call. Don't get too excited by a single gobble; even a tom with hens may respond to a locator call with a single response. Search for a bird that responds to every call you make. He's a prime candidate.

When you find such a bird, get within 200 yards in open country, half that distance in timber; sit down and get ready before you make a single hen call. Many hunters have been caught flat-footed when a hot-to-trot 2-year-old gobbler ran to their first yelp. Call just often enough to keep the bird gobbling, so you know where he is. If he holds his ground, sneak closer, if possible, or slip around to one side and call from your new position. If the bird

TYPICAL RUN-AND-GUN SCENARIO

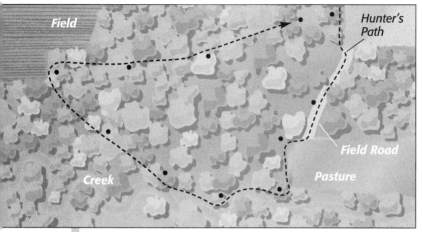

Field

Hunter's
Path

Field Road

Creek

Pasture

FOLLOW the easiest route to cover the most ground in the least amount of time when running and gunning. Skirt the edges of all openings and call every 100 to 200 yards, until you get a response.

continues to gobble in response to your calls, but moves steadily away, determine his direction and attempt to get ahead of him. If he moves steadily in your direction, call sparingly and stay ready.

If the area you're hunting has few mature toms, or if hens are abundant, the run-and-gun approach is usually a waste of time. A better option is to pick a good feeding spot and wait patiently for a flock of hungry birds to arrive.

This sit-and-wait tactic is most successful if you know the area well enough to predict travel routes. This is fairly easy in farm country where turkeys often frequent the same fields at approximately the same times daily. Locating turkey feeding areas is more difficult in big timber, but identifying travel routes is fairly simple. In deep woods, turkeys travel open hardwood bottoms, underbrush-free ridges and logging roads. Setting up along one of these known travel routes and calling sparingly is an excellent option for enlivening the dead zone. A blind can be a real asset when playing this waiting game, as can a decoy or two.

TYPICAL SIT-AND-WAIT SCENARIO

SIT AND WAIT for birds where you can cover locations where birds enter or exit fields (1), pastures (2) or other openings. Be patient, call sparingly and stay alert.

Patience is the key. Turkeys feed at midmorning, and a feeding flock is in no hurry, covering only about 200 yards per hour, on average.

LATE MORNING

Things begin to change in the spring turkey woods by about 10 a.m. After breeding and filling their crops, hens begin to wander from the tom and toward nesting areas. The pompous gobbler, suddenly bereft of female companionship, is again susceptible to calling. As any experienced turkey hunter can tell you, this is the best time to call a mature gobbler, because this is when they are most likely to be alone.

Cover lots of territory after 10 a.m. Use locator calls and loud cutting to elicit gobbles. In some parts of the country, hunting at this time of day is best done from a vehicle. You can cover more ground by vehicle than on foot. Stop every 1/4 mile or so to use your locator call. If a vehicle is not practical, start walking.

Locator calls are better than hen calls for prompting a tom

to begin gobbling. Once you've elicited a shock gobble, set up and get ready to seduce the bird with your most authentic hen calls. If you begin by making hen yelps, a tom may arrive before you are prepared to deliver the proper greeting.

If you prefer to sit and wait for your bird, late morning is a good time to stake out strutting zones. Gobblers that have been deserted by hens frequently meander back to their strutting zones and will readily respond to calls.

AFTERNOON

Even in states where all-day hunting is allowed, many hunters head home by noon. But experienced hunters know that gobblers can still be taken in the afternoon, though it takes patience and a slightly different strategy.

In the early afternoon, it's best to do what turkeys also do during this period – feed and rest. Find a turkey hangout – a dusting area or feeding site – set out a decoy or two, relax against a big tree and give a few yelps every 15 minutes or so. If a gobbler comes to your call at this hour, he usually won't announce himself until within shooting range. Many hunters have been jarred from midday naps by tiptoeing gobblers shouting at close range.

Action picks up again in late afternoon, when turkeys begin actively feeding and, later, working toward the roost. Once again, running and gunning becomes your best option.

If you have located a roosting area, determine the most likely direction from which the birds will approach, then set up in their path. Do not hunt the actual roost site. It is unethical and frightens birds from the roost. If you haven't pinpointed a roosting area, spend the last hour of daylight covering ground and using a locator call. If you hear a gobbler, slip in close and work the bird with hen calls. Even if you don't get a shot, you'll sleep easy knowing where to continue the hunt in the morning.

Making the Shot

More turkeys are missed, not because of improper hunting techniques or poor calling, but because hunters fail to set up properly to make the shot. When a gobbler responds to your call, don't panic and plop down right where you stand; take a few extra moments to ensure that you will be in the best position for a clear shot when he approaches.

An ideal ambush site is the base of a large tree located at the edge of a small clearing in which the tom can strut. The tree should be at least as wide as your shoulders, so it breaks your outline, and the open area should be no more than 50 yards wide. Larger clearings are more difficult to hunt because a gobbler typically approaches only far enough to be visible to the hen he hears calling. As soon as he enters the clearing, he'll often begin strutting until the hen comes to him.

If no clearings are available, try to find a tree overlooking good shooting lanes in several directions. Clear leaves and debris from your sitting area so you can shift position if necessary without making noise. Sit with your back against the tree, your knees up so you can rest your gun on them at a level shooting height. Angle your left shoulder (right-handed hunter) in the direction you last heard the bird. This will allow you to cover a 180-degree arc with minimal movement.

Estimate or use a range finder to calculate distances to various objects within 40 yards of your location. When a turkey appears, use its position relative to these objects to estimate its distance. Now get comfortable; you may have to hold your position for a long time.

If a bird gobbles consistently as he approaches, maintaining a fix on his location is easy. However, if he gobbles only sporadically or comes in quietly, you will need to depend upon hearing his footsteps in dry leaves or on visual confirmation to track his progress. Cautiously shift your body and adjust your point of aim as the bird approaches. Make final adjustments with your gun barrel only when the tom's head is obscured by a tree or his own fanned tail.

If the bird approaches from behind or at an angle that makes it difficult to shoot, don't try to whirl around and snap off a shot – a turkey's reactions are quicker than

SETTING UP FOR THE SHOT

SELECT a good tree to sit against and get in proper position; then (1) identify objects at the edge of effective shooting range. (2) Call just enough to keep the bird coming. (3) Shift your gun

yours. Instead, sit motionless and wait for the bird to move into a better shooting location. If he walks out of sight, shift into a better position, then call to draw him back into range.

Ideal shooting range is no more than 40 yards, but try not to let the bird get closer than 20 yards. Too close and, despite the best camouflage, a turkey is likely to detect you.

Fire only when the bird's head and neck are fully exposed, aiming at a spot midway down the neck. Don't shoot when the bird is strutting, because his neck is not fully exposed. Either wait for the tom to break strut on his own

into position when the gobbler's vision is obstructed by brush, trees or its own fanned tail. (4) When the bird goes down, hurry out to secure your trophy and be prepared for a quick follow-up shot.

or use a single alarm putt to cause him to break strut. As soon as he extends his neck to look for danger, shoot.

After your shot, immediately prepare to shoot again in case the bird attempts to run or fly away. If he goes down, run to him quickly. But do not pick him up until he is done kicking. Many hunters have been spurred by "dead" turkeys.

HOW TO DRAW A BOW ON A TURKEY

USE a large tree to break up your outline when bowhunting turkeys without benefit of a blind. Do not attempt to draw when the bird is in the open.

WAIT until the gobbler's head is behind a tree or other obstruction before smoothly coming to full draw. Turkeys are notoriously adept at detecting the slightest movement.

AIM at the spot where you expect the turkey to reappear. When the gobbler steps out from behind the obstruction, you should be in perfect position to shoot.

Spot & Stalk

USE *a spotting scope or high-powered binoculars to determine if there is a tom in the group you have spotted.*

The spot-and-stalk method of hunting turkeys can be extremely dangerous and should only be employed by veteran hunters in open country when they have positively identified a bearded gobbler. Stalking turkey sounds can result in shooting other hunters. Always thoroughly check backgrounds before shooting a stalked gobbler. A camouflaged hunter may have been calling the same bird you are stalking. He could be sitting just beyond the bird when you shoot.

Spot and stalk works best where turkeys frequent open habitat such as fields, pastures, open foothills and mountain meadows. Binoculars of at least 7x are best for spotting turkeys at a distance. A 15x to 45x spotting scope helps identify gobblers. In the West, a rifle hunter's only objective after spotting the turkey is to get within reasonable range, about 100 yards.

Some hunters prefer this method for saving time; if you can spot one or more gobblers before beginning to hunt, you're less likely to waste hours calling to birds that aren't there. The spot-and-stalk technique is also effective during midmorning hours when gobbling activity trails off and toms are feeding in open fields.

Pick a high vantage from which to glass. Some hunters carry screw-in steps so they can climb trees to gain height. In the West, where it is often necessary to cover many miles in search of turkeys, hunters often rely on four-wheel-drive vehicles to reach vantage points. Scan open fields, pastures, CRP fields, meadows and open prairie. Scrutinize any dark spot. A strutting tom looks like a large, black ball.

Once you spot turkeys, try to determine their sex – you don't want to waste time stalking hens. Toms usually fan their tails every 5 to 15 minutes, but if they don't, use a spotting scope to check for beards.

Before charging after birds, plan a route that takes advantage of all natural and man-made features to conceal your approach. Since turkeys are nearly always on the move, watch them long enough to determine their direction of travel before beginning the stalk.

As you stalk, resist the urge to constantly peek at the gobbler. Unless spooked, turkeys feed at a casual pace. Constantly trying to keep visual tabs on your quarry is risky business.

If the bird has moved out of sight and does not respond to calling within 15 minutes, go after him, continuing in the direction you suspect he went. Call every 100 yards. Don't hurry. Unless you have spooked the bird, he will not be far away.

Once you have slipped within range, double-check your target and the surrounding area to make sure the bird is legal and there are no other hunters around. Then shoot.

Again, never forget how dangerous stalking can be. You will be calling and crawling within shotgun range of real birds. You could easily be mistaken for a gobbler. Consider wearing a large swatch of blaze orange on your back. Turkeys in front of you are unlikely to see it, but other hunters might. Ideally, you should stalk within calling range of birds, then sweet-talk them to you.

SPOT-AND-STALK TIPS

SPOTTING SCOPES
of at least 15x
help to determine
the sex of a bird
you have located.

SCREW-IN TREE
STEPS make it
easy to get high
enough to obtain
a good view of
open areas.

FOLDS AND
CREASES in the
land provide super
access routes for
hunters to sneak
up on unsuspect-
ing birds.

Hunting with a Partner

Although turkey hunting is generally considered a solo endeavor, hunting with a partner has its advantages.

A pair of experienced turkey hunters can cooperate to solve one of turkey hunting's toughest challenges – the hung-up tom (p. 140). Some wary gobblers refuse to move any closer than 60 yards to a caller. They strut and gobble just out of range, demanding that the "hen" go to them. To prevent this, a shooter should set up at the usual distance from a calling gobbler while the caller hangs back 30 to 100 yards.

The distance the caller stays back is determined by the surrounding habitat. The more open the country, the more distance between caller and shooter. Make sure you and your partner know each other's location at all times. When the shooter is in position, the caller goes to work, and the gobbler responds the same way he has done countless times before: He strides to within 75 yards or so of the caller and starts to strut, waiting for a hen to join him. Preoccupied with his breeding display, the tom rarely sees the shooter.

But remember, we are talking about two veteran turkey hunters. When either of the hunters is a novice, safety demands that the novice stick close to the more experienced hunter. In fact, one of the best ways to learn to work turkeys is to sit shoulder-to-shoulder with an experienced hunter while he does the calling.

Two partners can double their odds for "roosting" birds by scouting in different directions. The next morning, both cooperate to hunt the most likely bird discovered.

Partners can also assist one another during stalks. While one moves toward the birds, the other keeps an eye on them through binoculars. If the stalker loses track of them, he can look back to his partner, who can hand-signal directions.

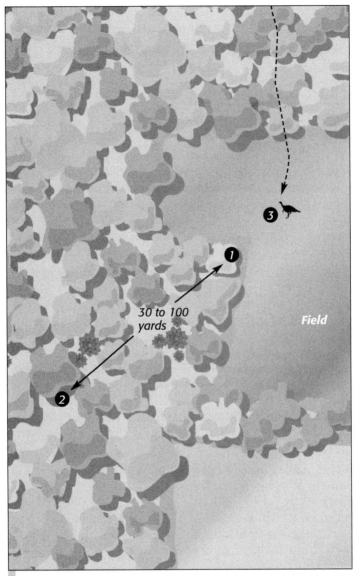

TYPICAL TAG-TEAM SETUP positions the shooter (1) 30 to 100 yards in front of the caller (2). If a gobbler (3) hangs up short of the caller, the bird will be within range of the shooter.

TAG-TEAM TIPS

CALL-SHY TOMS can sometimes be fooled by one hunter remaining in position while the other slowly walks away, making occasional hen calls.

TWO HUNTERS calling side by side can easily imitate a flock of turkeys. This tactic may coax a gobbler accustomed to hearing a single caller.

Float-Hunting

Want to really throw a wise old gobbler a curve ball? Try float-hunting. Approaching by water is sometimes the best way to reach turkeys that rarely hear an artificial call. In areas that see heavy hunting pressure, toms grow accustomed to hunters approaching from the same directions; a hunter who slips in by water often gets a much warmer reception from those call-shy birds.

Consider the float-hunting option in any turkey habitat bordered by streams, rivers, reservoirs or large lakes. Tens of thousands of acres of public land are accessible from water, including state and national forests, wildlife management areas, national wildlife refuges and Army Corp of Engineers holdings. On private lands, you'll need the owner's permission to hunt.

Choose a craft suited to the waters you'll be hunting. A bass boat is ideal on large lakes or reservoirs, since it is roomy enough to hold all your gear, speedy enough to cover a lot of water, and has a shallow draft to slip into secluded bays and coves without scraping bottom.

On small rivers, a jon boat rigged with a small outboard is tough to beat. On many streams, a canoe is ideal for silently slipping up on turkeys. Aluminum boats are rugged, but noisy. Before using an aluminum boat to float-hunt turkeys, soundproof it (following page).

On a large reservoir or lake, the best way to locate a gobbler is to motor slowly into every bay you come to, cut the outboard, wait a minute or two and then blow a locator call. If a turkey answers, pinpoint his position, beach the boat and move in.

Hunting on rivers and streams is best accomplished by two hunters, each with a vehicle. Drive to a predetermined take-out location, and leave one vehicle. Then drive to the launch site with your boat. Blow a locator call every few

hundred yards as you float along. Avoid calling near rapids or riffles, where the sound of running water can obscure the call of a responding gobbler.

Don't try to cover too much country when float-hunting. In good turkey habitat, a float of only a few miles should be enough to put you onto gobblers.

Don't overlook islands on larger lakes, rivers and reservoirs. Many islands are home to small populations of turkeys. Odds are good that island gobblers have never even heard a fake turkey call.

Maps can be critical to the success of a float hunt. Helpful maps include: navigational charts of the waterway you are hunting, a map that plainly shows all public land adjoining the waterway and an aerial photograph or topographical map of the area. Make special note of secluded coves, backwaters and creek mouths that provide access to turkey habitat. Areas difficult to access from land are especially likely to offer good hunting.

TAG-TEAM TIPS

SOUNDPROOF your boat by covering the bottom with old carpeting to muffle the bangs and clangs that spook gobblers. Wrap the gunnels of a metal boat with foam pipe covering to deaden potential gobbler-spooking noises.

USE a seaworthy boat to reach untouched pockets of birds on many of the large southern reservoirs.

SNEAK into secluded coves and bays to locate turkeys in a boat equipped with an electric trolling motor.

SPECIAL
SITUATIONS

Barriers

Wild turkeys can easily fly or walk across creeks, roads, ravines and other barriers, and they readily do so to reach feeding or roosting areas. But when responding to calls, toms are notorious for stopping cold when they reach the same barriers. A shallow ditch or a rickety fence can be enough to stop a gobbler dead in its tracks.

BARRIERS, such as this stream, often prevent a gobbler from continuing toward a hunter's calls, even though the bird could easily fly across it if he chose. The best way to avoid this problem is to set up in a position where the gobbler won't have to cross barriers.

The best solution to this problem is to avoid it in the first place. Good preseason scouting helps you pinpoint all possible barriers. When hunting unfamiliar ground, survey your surroundings before setting up to call. If there is a potential barrier between you and the bird, relocate before beginning to call.

No matter how careful you are, if you hunt turkeys long enough you'll eventually find yourself facing the formidable task of trying to call a gobbler across a barrier. If a tom refuses to cross a barrier despite your best calling, shut up. Sudden silence sometimes makes a tom curious enough to cross the barrier. In most cases, though, the gobbler will gradually lose interest and walk away. When this happens, quickly move to a better position and begin working the bird again.

TYPICAL BARRIER SITUATIONS

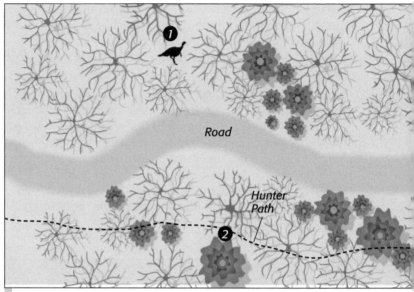

ROADS that see a fair amount of traffic act as barriers to gobblers coming to a call. Instead of trying to call the bird (1) to

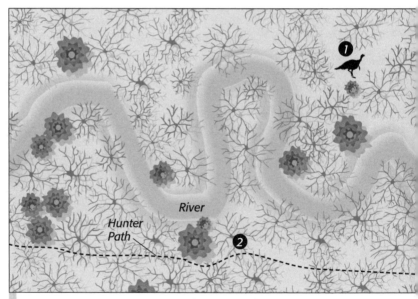

STREAMS OR RIVERS are rarely crossed by birds responding to a call. Don't try to call the bird (1) across the stream to you (2).

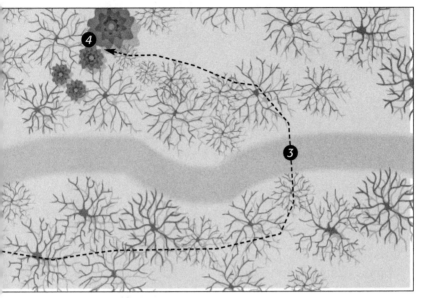

*your position across the road (2), cross the road in a spot (3)
where he cannot see you, and set up in a new position (4).*

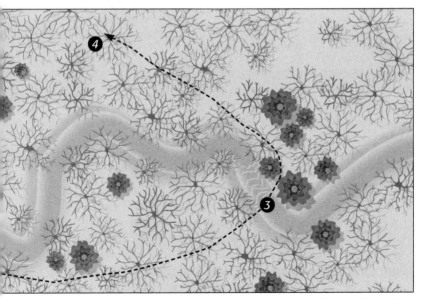

*Find a place where you can cross (3) and work the bird from his
side of the stream (4).*

Hung-Up Gobblers

If toms that respond to your calls often hang up before they reach shooting range, it's time to reconsider how you set up.

Novices tend to set up so they'll be able to see turkeys coming from a long distance. That's wrong.

Experienced hunters know a tom will approach only so far before he expects to see the hen tempting him with her calls. If a gobbler's view is unobstructed, his inclination is to stop at 75 to 100 yards, begin strutting, and wait for the hen to approach him. If he sees nothing, he gets suspicious and often refuses to come any closer.

Prevent this predicament by setting up in a smaller open area so that the tom will be in range when he steps into view. You can also sit behind an obstruction so a gobbler is forced to come close before he sees there is no hen to court. One ideal setup is to position yourself 15 to 30 yards over the crest of a ridge on the side opposite the tom. When he pops over the knoll for a look, you'll have a perfect shot, although you may not be able to see his beard.

Another excellent way to sidestep the problem is to use the tag-team approach with two hunters (p. 126). A similar approach is to set up just inside the brushy fringes along a curve in a logging road. A gobbler responding to your calling will follow the curve as he tries to find an open area where his strutting will be visible to hens.

Unfortunately, habitat and terrain don't always provide these locations. In grasslands and in open hardwoods with little underbrush, for example, it's difficult if not impossible to find a narrow view. What then?

The first impulse is to call more often and more aggressively, but that rarely works. The gobbler already believes a hen is close. He doesn't want to hear more from her, he wants to see her. A better option, and one that requires steady nerves, is to remain silent and wait. Patience, not calling skill, is the key to killing a hung-up gobbler in open habitat.

If you remain quiet, the tom should eventually stop strutting and either drift away in search of new hen or come sneaking in to look for the stubborn hen he heard just minutes earlier.

A tom that chooses to look for you may take his time. He'll take a step or two, look and listen, take another few steps. You may wait 15 to 20 minutes before you even know he is still in the area. He'll be exceedingly alert and cautious, and will spot the slightest movement, so don't twitch. Scan the surroundings by moving your eyes, not your head. You may get lucky and hear the tom walking in the leaves before he comes into view, but more often he'll appear without warning. If your gun is not already in position, you're out of luck.

If the gobbler doesn't show up after 20 minutes, chances are good he gave up on you and walked away. But don't write him off quite yet. Walk to the spot where you last saw or heard him, and blow a locator call. If the tom gobbles, determine where he is and where he is most likely headed, then circle to get ahead of him. Now you can play the game again. This time, try to pick a setup where the gobbler will be in range when you first see him. And use a different call than the one you used the first time; turkeys get suspicious if they hear the same tune played over and over.

Another trick for drawing a hung-up gobbler within shooting range is to use decoys (p. 61). In many cases, a gobbler that spots a hen decoy is reassured enough to come closer. The technique is not infallible, however. Some toms play hard-to-get even if they see a decoy. They still expect the hen to close those final few yards. These characters can often be fooled by propping a jake decoy near the fake hen. The idea that any hen would stay with a jake rather than rush toward the old master is too much. The old boy usually runs in to thrash the upstart male, and then you've got him.

TIPS FOR WORKING HUNG-UP GOBBLERS

POSITION yourself behind a large deadfall. A tom will usually approach close enough to see beyond the tree, giving you a good shot.

SCRATCH in the leaves to mimic the sound of a hen feeding. To a hung-up gobbler, this suggests a hen has lost interest in him. Unable to stand being shunned, some toms break strut and come to find the feeding hen.

Open Fields

Even in areas with plentiful woodlands, turkeys spend a lot of time in pastures, agricultural fields and Conservation Reserve Program (CRP) lands.

Open fields are attractive to turkeys because they provide both food and protection. Mature turkeys have little to fear from avian predators, and they can easily spot ground-hunting predators.

Rain and wind also cause turkeys to seek open areas. Why they choose open fields when it is raining is anyone's guess, but when it's windy they probably see and hear better in the open than in noisy woods. Rustling leaves camouflage predator footsteps, and dancing branches

confound a turkey's usually sharp eyesight. Regardless of the weather, toms gravitate to open fields whenever they lose track of hens.

While a gobbler with hens is almost impossible to call from an open field, a solitary tom is a prime candidate for the call. Once you spot an open-field gobbler, set up as close to the edge of the field and the gobbler as possible.

Forget trying to set up a decoy. If you can see the gobbler, he'll spot you if you try to erect a decoy in the field. Just get as close as you can, and trust that your calling will bring the bird within range.

Begin by making a few soft, contented clucks and purrs. Sudden loud calling may startle the gobbler right out of the field. You can always increase volume, if necessary. If the gobbler begins to walk or strut in your direction, keep up the low-key muttering, but if he ignores you, throw in a series of quiet yelps.

Gobblers often strut for hours in open fields, moving slowly and almost reluctantly toward a call. Pick out a rock, tree or dirt clump between you and a strutting gobbler, and use it to gauge his forward progress. As long as he's advancing, no matter how slowly, just keep him interested with soft calling. It may take him an hour to cover 100 yards, but if you're patient, he'll eventually strut into range.

If your best efforts fail, try again on a later day. Turkeys often use the same fields about the same time each day. They also tend to enter the field at the same location each time, often via an old logging road or farm lane. An open gate is another excellent bet. If you've identified such an entry route, stake it out the next time you hunt.

Range estimation is difficult in open fields, and many hunters shoot at birds that are out of range. To prevent this, use a range finder, or pick out an object in the field which you determine to be at your maximum range. This marker serves as your reference point for determining when the bird is within range.

TIPS FOR HUNTING OPEN FIELDS

FARM LANES or logging roads leading to crop fields are repeatedly used by turkeys entering fields. A decoy along such a route can cause a tom to stop and strut, giving you an excellent shot.

PASTURES mean cows, and cows mean cow pies. Turkeys love to stroll through pastures and kick over cow pies for insects hiding there.

Hunting for Prairie Birds

INCREASING NUMBERS of eastern hunters are traveling to western states such as South Dakota, Nebraska and Kansas to hunt for Merriam's and Rio Grande turkeys. Referred to as "prairie birds" because of the environment in which they live, these gobblers often present special problems for hunters accustomed to hunting the big woods for eastern turkeys. While the same calls and calling techniques work on turkeys anywhere, regardless of subspecies, successfully hunting prairie birds often means readjusting your hunting tactics and mental attitude.

For years, prairie gobblers were considered inferior second cousins of "real" turkeys. This was because, until recently, prairie birds were only lightly hunted. Hunting pressure is what makes a wild turkey wary. But things have changed. Today, prairie birds are seeing more and more hunting pressure. Anyone who underestimates prairie birds today is in for a rude awakening.

Prairie birds can be placed into two categories: one, we'll call "creek-bottom turkeys," and the other, "nomad turkeys." Creek-bottom turkeys refuse to leave the thinly timbered creek and river bottoms. They follow the skimpiest side drainages as long as they support a few scattered trees, but they rarely leave the creek bottoms or wander barren prairies. This trait of sticking to timber makes creek-bottom gobblers fairly predictable. Even if you have not found a gobbling bird to work, setting up in a funnel and waiting for birds to pass works well. Where the creeks have enough water, float-hunting is an excellent way to cover lots of ground.

Nomad turkeys, on the other hand, are real travelers; they think nothing of wandering prairie, miles from the nearest tree. These birds live in restricted creek and river-bottom drainages, maybe only a half mile in length. But they don't confine themselves to this ribbon of habitat; instead, they strike off for the day, wandering far and wide, but religiously return to the same roost each evening. This makes finding the birds each morning a snap; but once they are off the roost and wandering, you'll have to cover a lot of ground to find them. Best tactics include scanning for birds from a nearby high spot and planning a route to intercept them, or setting up a few hundred yards from the roost tree to work the birds as they make their way to the roost.

The days of easy hunts on prairie birds are coming to an end.

Call-Shy Birds

Turkey hunting is growing rapidly. As increasing numbers of sportsmen fall victim to "turkey fever," gobblers on public land endure a barrage of calling, both good and bad. Nothing makes a gobbler as call-shy as consistent, bungled hunting pressure and endless calling.

In areas where turkeys are heavily hunted, your chances for luring call-shy toms can be improved if you change your calling pattern. If all else fails, the best strategy can be to simply put away your calls.

A gobbler already in the company of females, for example, is reluctant to give up hens in order to pursue a will-o'-the-wisp bird in the bush. Pursuing a tom with hens requires considerable finesse (p. 152). Toms also tend to be quiet and call-shy late in the season, when gobbling activity naturally begins to taper off.

When faced with shy toms, some hunters try to outcall every other hunter in the woods. Such an approach virtually guarantees failure, since hard-hunted gobblers have learned that loud calling signifies danger.

When hunting pressured toms, make it a rule to call sparingly and softly. Stick to quiet clucks and purrs, the sounds made by contented, feeding hens. Rake the leaves with your hand to mimic the sounds of hens scratching for food. Be patient and remain alert. Call-shy toms often arrive unannounced.

Don't approach a gobbler you hear from the easiest, most obvious direction. You can bet every other hunter who has heard the bird has done just that. Instead, walk a little farther and come at him from an unusual direction.

In heavily hunted areas, you're well advised to carry a wide selection of calls – not just your favorite standbys. Pay attention to the calls other hunters are using. If the diaphragm call, for instance, is the most popular, then use a box, tube, slate or push-pull call; something a local may not have heard before. Many hunters make the mistake of assuming that if a gobbler is going to respond, he will respond to any call; but that is not true. Try them all, and don't be afraid to experiment.

Your chances for success also improve if you hunt when others don't. In bad weather, few hunters are in the woods, and toms often relax. Where all-day hunting is legal, try hunting in late morning or afternoon, when most hunters have called it quits.

If calling proves to be unproductive despite your best efforts, put away your calls and rely strictly on knowledge, hunch and patience. Sit along a field edge, woods road or ridge line, and just wait. If birds show up but are just out of range, don't touch those calls, no matter how tempting. Instead, use your hand or a stick to rustle in the leaves. A gobbler that hears you may assume the sound is made by hens feeding and wander over to check things out.

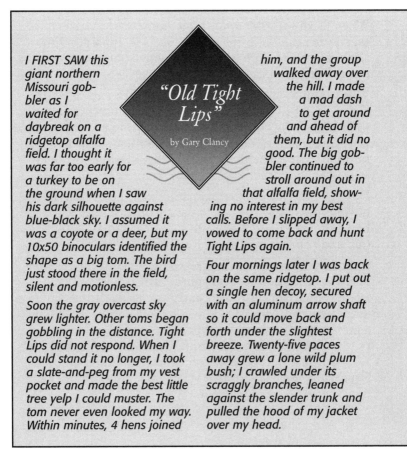

"Old Tight Lips"

by Gary Clancy

I FIRST SAW this giant northern Missouri gobbler as I waited for daybreak on a ridgetop alfalfa field. I thought it was far too early for a turkey to be on the ground when I saw his dark silhouette against blue-black sky. I assumed it was a coyote or a deer, but my 10x50 binoculars identified the shape as a big tom. The bird just stood there in the field, silent and motionless.

Soon the gray overcast sky grew lighter. Other toms began gobbling in the distance. Tight Lips did not respond. When I could stand it no longer, I took a slate-and-peg from my vest pocket and made the best little tree yelp I could muster. The tom never even looked my way. Within minutes, 4 hens joined him, and the group walked away over the hill. I made a mad dash to get around and ahead of them, but it did no good. The big gobbler continued to stroll around out in that alfalfa field, showing no interest in my best calls. Before I slipped away, I vowed to come back and hunt Tight Lips again.

Four mornings later I was back on the same ridgetop. I put out a single hen decoy, secured with an aluminum arrow shaft so it could move back and forth under the slightest breeze. Twenty-five paces away grew a lone wild plum bush; I crawled under its scraggly branches, leaned against the slender trunk and pulled the hood of my jacket over my head.

Decoys can be effective on quiet gobblers that have had numerous run-ins with hunters. A tom fearful of answering a call will often commit himself if he receives the visual confirmation of a decoy.

As a last resort, put the sneak on them. Many hunters believe that a turkey's eyes and ears are so keen that trying to stalk within shotgun range is futile, but this is not true. If you are careful, move slowly, and take advantage of all cover and terrain features, you stand a good chance of sneaking within shooting range of a gobbler. Just keep your hands off your calls and keep your eyes open for other hunters.

A steady rain had been falling all night, and, knowing that turkeys usually remain on the roost longer on rainy mornings, I settled in for what I anticipated to be a long wait.

My mistake. The big gobbler materialized without warning, his fist-sized white head glowing like a child's nightlight in the predawn gloom. The bird strolled up to my decoy, an old favorite I call "Matilda." All I could do was watch. My Knight muzzleloading shotgun lay sprawled across my lap. I couldn't make a move without the gobbler spotting me.

True to his name, Old Tight Lips never once gobbled as he began to strut for Matilda. When the tom's head was momentarily blocked behind his fanned tail, I managed to get the shotgun nearly to my shoulder. Then the gobbler sidled up to the decoy and started to pirouette. His wing nudged the decoy's tail, and Matilda spun around and smacked him in the head. As the surprised gobbler came to full attention, I inched the buttplate to my shoulder and snuggled down on the stock. The gobbler's big head was directly behind Matilda's, but there was no time to wait. I touched the trigger. Flames leaped and smoke billowed in the calm Missouri air. I jumped to my feet and raced to find the gobbler dead behind the still spinning decoy.

The big gobbler weighed 26½ pounds, sported an 11½-inch beard and 1⅝-inch hooked spurs.

Oh yes, Matilda had taken 23 copper-plated #5s in the line of duty.

Gobbler with Hens

During the spring breeding season, toms in the company of hens are reluctant to come to a call for obvious reasons: they're already busy with breeding partners. This is one of the most common and frustrating obstacles confronting spring turkey hunters.

Often this problem is as difficult to diagnose as to solve. Occasionally, you'll actually see hens with a gobbler, but,

TURKEY HUNTERS in the southern states refer to a gobbler with hens as being "all henned up." But no matter where you hunt, a tom in the company of hens represents one of the most difficult challenges in spring turkey hunting.

more often, you must deduce this fact from vocal cues. For example, if you hear a tom gobbling freely on the roost but notice that he falls silent immediately after fly-down, it's a good bet he has joined a hen. Or, if you establish a dialogue with a tom but notice that his gobbling grows steadily more distant, it's likely a hen is leading him away from what she believes to be a competing hen. Similarly, if his calls seem to come from random directions with no obvious movement pattern, he's probably following a group of feeding hens. This tom may gobble in response to your calls, but is unlikely to come looking for a mystery hen when he already has the real thing.

One solution to this problem is to give up calling to the gobbler – call to the hen, instead. A hen will sometimes

behave in a jealous and protective fashion when she hears another hen competing for her mate's attention. If a hen answers your call, respond immediately with the same call she used. Match her, yelp for yelp, cluck for cluck, until you sense she is growing agitated. Then interrupt her in mid-yelp with a loud yelp of your own. The goal is to make the hen angry or curious enough to come looking for you – hopefully, with the gobbler in tow.

Since a gobbler in the company of hens usually lags behind, you must lure the flock close without spooking them. Don't be discouraged if you lose a few birds this way. Even the best camouflage may not save you when a hen is within a few feet of your position.

If you can't break the gobbler away from the hens or lure the hens to you, the next option is to ambush the gobbler. Stop calling, and try to determine the direction the birds

AMBUSHING A GOBBLER WITH HENS

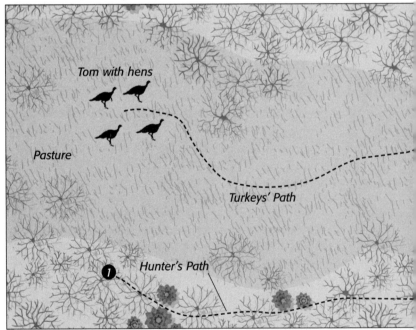

Tom with hens

Pasture

Turkeys' Path

Hunter's Path

AMBUSH a tom with hens when he won't respond to your calls. Farm field roads, logging trails, creek bottoms and open draws all funnel feeding turkeys along a predictable route. Once you

are traveling, using binoculars if necessary. Turkeys have a natural tendency to follow the easiest path when feeding. If they are moving along a farm lane, logging trail, creek bottom or other obvious route, carefully loop around to get in front of them, and sit tight until the tom pulls within range.

An option few hunters use during spring hunting is to rush the birds and scatter a flock. If you can get no closer than 75 to 100 yards, charge the flock to scatter it. The idea is to separate the tom from the hens. Within an hour or so, he'll grow lonely and may respond to your calling.

Sometimes the best strategy is to leave a gobbler and his hens and search for a solo tom. A difficult decision, to be sure, but console yourself with the knowledge that you can find this tom again. Remember where you last saw him. An hour or two after his hens have gone to nest, he might be ready to pay attention to you.

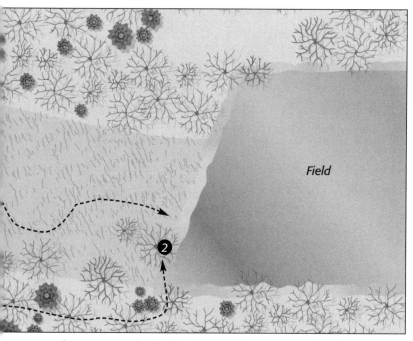

have spotted the birds and determined in which direction they are heading (1), sneak ahead of them, set up in a new location (2), and let them come to you.

155

Bad Weather

TURKEYS *often abandon woods during windy and rainy weather in favor of open fields, where they can see and hear better.*

A turkey hunter who insists on waiting for perfect weather won't hunt much – spring weather is just too fickle. Rain, wind, snow, fog, freezing temperatures and blistering heat are all possible during a single spring turkey season. The best advice is to hunt whenever you can, adjusting tactics to conditions. Hunters who brave unpleasant weather often increase their chances for success because the competition stays indoors.

In many cases, you won't need to adust your strategy at all. Heat doesn't bother turkeys, nor does a cold snap, even if it includes a freak spring snowstorm. Fog may cause turkeys to remain on the roost later in the morning, which can work in your favor. Rain and wind do cause turkeys to alter daily patterns, forcing hunters to adjust tactics accordingly.

Rain generally drives turkeys to open areas. A heavy downpour may push them under canopy cover, but gentle, all-day rains don't seem to bother them. They'll spend most of their time in open fields and pastures. Knowing this, you can glass open areas, instead of slogging through dripping woods.

Once you locate birds, get as close as you can before setting up to call. When toms are reluctant to come to the call, such as when they are with hens, you may be better off not calling at all. Instead, set up along the field edge for an ambush.

Wind doesn't spook turkeys in the same way it does whitetailed deer, but it can cause gobblers to abandon common haunts in favor of calmer places. A strong wind whipping

AMBUSHING A GOBBLER WITH HENS

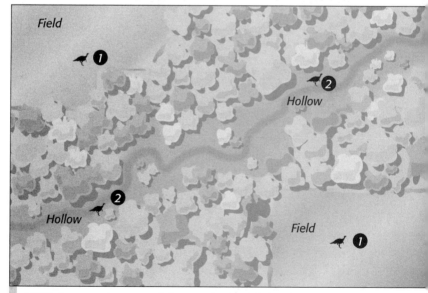

WIND forces turkeys out of the woods toward open areas (1) and into open hollows (2) tucked out of the wind. Don't waste time looking anywhere else when the wind is blowing over 20 mph.

branches about creates enough noise to impair a turkey's hearing. Wind-lashed branches and bushes compromise the bird's ability to respond to sudden motions. Under these conditions, turkeys are vulnerable to predators. They respond by moving to open areas or sheltered hollows out of the wind. Look for them there.

On windy days, both you and your quarry will have difficulty hearing. Call with as much volume as you can muster, and when a tom gobbles a response, sit down, raise your gun and get ready – anytime you hear a gobble on a windy day, the bird is probably close.

TIPS FOR TAKING TURKEYS IN BAD WEATHER

STORE box and slate calls in resealable plastic bags when hunting in rain.

WAIT for turkeys to fly down from the roost an hour or two later than normal when hunting on foggy mornings.

Rainy-Day Gobblers

WALTER PARROT, a champion turkey caller from Missouri, has won just about every award possible in the world of big-time calling contests. Unfortunately, his job as a bricklayer doesn't let him hunt anytime he pleases.

"On sunny days I'm working," he states, "but you can't lay bricks in the rain, so whenever the weather turns foul, I go hunting. In some ways, I think locating and calling in gobblers is easier in the rain than on those beautiful spring mornings we all pray for."

His theory is this: On bright, sunny days, odds are good that most toms will start gobbling on their own off the roost, attracting hens. Chances are excellent these gobblers will saunter off with those hens. But when it is raining, most turkeys sleep in. Without hens to compete against, your odds for locating a gobbler, then calling it in, are excellent.

"Sometimes I know there are turkeys within hearing range, but they just refuse to gobble," Walter says. "But if I can't get one to sound off, I don't worry about it, because I know where to look for those birds when they fly down."

Most hunters think turkeys stay in the woods when it is raining, but they don't. Instead, the birds head for open fields, where they can use their senses better and not get their feathers soaking wet by dragging through the vegetation. Pastures and low-cut alfalfa fields are their favorites.

Fall Hunting

Many states have a fall turkey season. Since spring turkey hunting tactics are based upon the mating ritual and turkeys do not breed in fall, spring tactics are of little use. The name of the game is to appeal to the wild turkey's gregarious nature. In fall, hens and their young-of-the-year gather in flocks of a dozen to 100 birds. Mature gobblers hang out in small bachelor groups of two to seven. A few mature toms spend the fall months alone. Since either sex is legal during autumn, most hunters key on the easier to locate and call hens and juvenile birds.

There is little gobbling at this season. In fact, fall flocks don't say much at all. For most of the day, they only purr and cluck as they feed, and these soft sounds don't carry

far. The crashings of their big feet, however, do. Fall flocks spend a lot of time scratching through leaves looking for nuts, green plants, seeds and insects. On a quiet day when the leaves are dry you can hear them from 100 yards or more. Never crest a ridge before first stopping to listen for turkeys scratching on the other side.

Once you locate a flock, rush it or send a dog to split it up. The more fragmented the flock, the better. Lonely individuals will be that much easier to call. Once the flock has been scattered, set up near the dispersal site, wait 5 or 10 minutes, and begin to call. Yelps and kee-kees are the best fall calls. Because the flock has a strong bond, the birds will quickly try to regroup. It is not unusual to hear birds calling to each other from all directions when a flock has been broken.

Hunting fall turkeys with a dog is rare but nothing new. For well over a century, fall hunters have relied upon "man's best friend" to help them find and scatter fall flocks. Where this tactic is legal, most hunters simply take a bird dog or house pet along on the hunt and hope "Old Rover" does more good than harm. Real aficionados, however, use specially trained turkey dogs.

A turkey dog is expected to hunt for the scent trail of a flock, follow that scent, follow it to a flock, and then dash among the birds at full speed while barking excitedly to scatter them. Since some birds always choose to run instead of fly, a good turkey dog returns to the scatter site and trails each individual runner until it flushes. After every bird has been routed, the dog returns to its master and sits quietly. Then the hunter calls the scattered birds. Some turkey dogs are even trained to lie inside camouflaged sacks so that they don't spook returning turkeys.

Hunting specifically for a mature gobbler in fall is tough. Once spring breeding chores are behind them, gobblers hang out in small bachelor groups. Because there are few gobblers in any turkey population, just finding one in fall can be difficult. Find a gobbler band, however, and you can rush and scatter it just as you would a flock of hens and juveniles. But because gobblers are not as flock-oriented as hens and young turkeys, they are not as eager to regroup. It may take hours or even days before gobblers reconvene. Only hunters with extreme patience consistently take fall gobblers.

Once gobblers have been scattered, get comfortable near the scatter point, because you are in for a long wait. A blind helps. It is almost impossible to sit stone-still for hours at a time. Wait a half hour and then give a single gobbler cluck or coarse gobbler yelp. Don't call more often than once every half hour. And don't expect an approaching gobbler to announce his arrival. Fall gobblers come in quietly.

Unless you hear him walking in dry leaves, your first indication that he has arrived is when you see him or when he calls at close range. He knows he should be able to see the gobbler he has heard, and when he doesn't, he clucks or yelps himself to say, "O.K., buddy, I'm here; now where are you?" Odds are excellent that the gobbler will be in range when he clucks, so try not to jump in surprise.

Because mature gobblers are so unresponsive to the call during fall, many are taken by stand-hunters along well-used travel routes. Old logging roads, field edges and dry or partially dry creek beds are favored travel lanes for fall gobblers. Personal observation is the best way to determine where gobblers are likely to pass. Tracks and droppings are good sign.

TIPS FOR TAKING TURKEYS IN BAD WEATHER

DEER and turkeys often feed together. Some hunters believe the two species warn each other of danger.

DOGS trained specifically for fall turkey hunting increase your odds of scoring and add enjoyment to the hunt.

The Grand Slam

A hunter achieves the turkey *grand slam* by shooting each of the four major sub-species: the eastern, Merriam's, Rio Grande and Florida wild turkeys. Adding the Gould's is called the *royal slam*, and a hunter who adds the sixth subspecies, the Ocellated, has earned a *world slam*. But because the Gould's and Ocellated are found in such limited numbers, few hunters will ever have the opportunity to hunt them.

Each subspecies must be taken by legal methods,

Rio Grande

Eastern

Florida

Merriam's

of course, but other than this, there are few restrictions on qualifying for the grand slam. Hunters can use bows, shotguns, rifles or muzzleloaders. They can tag all four birds in a single year, or over a lifetime.

The first step toward completing a grand slam is to contact wildlife agencies in areas you want to hunt. These agencies will send you hunting regulations and instructions on how to apply for hunting permits. You can also contact state turkey biologists to learn which areas have high concentrations of turkeys and when peak gobbling occurs.

In states with considerable public land, contact the appropriate managing agency for maps and information. In regions with no public hunting land, your best option may be to contact a professional guide or commercial ranch that offers fee hunting. One of the best ways to find a hunt on private land is to look in the back of turkey hunting publications for guides advertising specialized hunts.

If possible, plan your hunts so you can pursue at least two subspecies. On a trip to Texas, for example, you might be able to hunt both Rio Grande and Merriam's turkeys in different parts of the state. In Florida, you can hunt eastern and Florida turkeys by driving only a few miles.

There is little need to vary your hunting strategy when working for the grand slam because tactics that work on one subspecies work on the others. Although the voices of the main subspecies are not identical, they are so close that there is no need to adjust your calling. Variations in hunting technique will usually be dictated by food sources, habitat and terrain – not subspecies. In southern Texas brush country, for example, wild turkeys roost in large flocks in rare, isolated oak groves. In Florida, turkeys prefer to roost in cypress trees over water, and in the West, they like ponderosa pines.

EASTERN WILD TURKEY

For the would-be grand slam hunter, this subspecies is often the first collected. Thanks to aggressive restoration programs, the eastern exists in good numbers over a broad range that includes many of the most populated areas of the country. And since this subspecies thrives on millions of acres of public land, hunting it need not be an expensive endeavor. There are also many fine commercial hunting operations that cater to turkey hunters in the eastern's range, especially in the southeastern states.

The eastern wild turkey is considered by well-traveled hunters to be the most difficult of all subspecies to call. This is not because the birds have greater inherent intelligence, but because eastern turkey populations are hunted more frequently than other subspecies, and consequently have more hens than gobblers.

FLORIDA WILD TURKEY

If the eastern is the easiest bird to collect, based on availability and sheer numbers, then the Florida subspecies is the most difficult. Numbering fewer than 100,000, this subspecies occupies a restricted range in a small portion of Florida. Opportunities to hunt on public land are limited, so the best odds for taking a Florida wild turkey are on private lands.

RIO GRANDE WILD TURKEY

Texas is home to about 85 percent of all Rio Grande turkeys, with the southern and central regions of the state holding the largest number. Rios are also found in parts of Oklahoma and Kansas. Nearly all Rio hunting is done on private ranches that charge fees.

MERRIAM'S WILD TURKEY

Regarded by many as the most striking subspecies, the Merriam's wild turkey is scattered across many of the western states. The Black Hills area of South Dakota is a popular destination because it offers 1.2 million acres of national forest land open to public hunting and is relatively close for eastern hunters. National forests in New Mexico and Arizona and Bureau of Land Management holdings in eastern Montana also provide excellent hunting.

Many ranches across this subspecies' range offer daily fee hunting, sometimes with room and board. Guided hunts are also an option if time is more precious than money.

CARE
OF YOUR BIRD

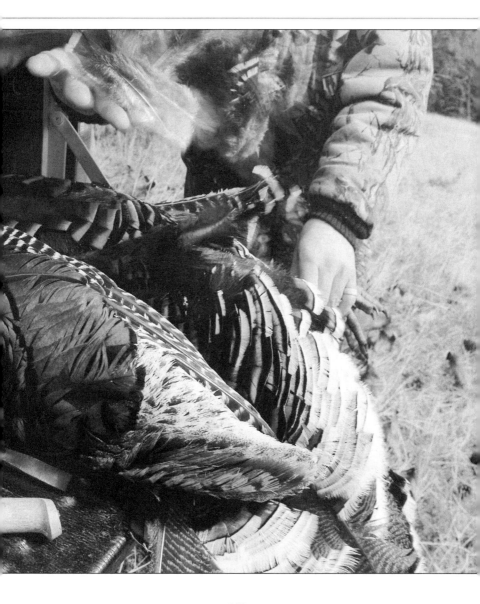

Preserving a Trophy

There are several ways to immortalize a successful turkey hunt. If you plan to have your turkey mounted, handle it with special care. Many hunters try to restrain a flopping turkey in an effort to protect the feathers, but this can break more feathers than it protects. Let the bird kick until dead, then pick up any dislodged feathers and place them in a plastic bag. The taxidermist can reattach these if they're critical to the bird's appearance.

Immediately stuff paper towels in the bird's throat and anus to prevent blood and other fluids from staining the feathers. Wait 5 to 10 minutes before handling the bird any further. A turkey's feathers are normally quite loose, but within a few minutes after death become harder to dislodge. Always handle a turkey by the legs or neck.

If possible, put the bird on ice or in a freezer within a few hours. Gutting is not necessary for taxidermy purposes but may improve meat quality if temperatures are high. If you must field-dress the bird, cut a small opening between the lower tip of the breast and the anus, and reach inside to remove the entrails. Avoid staining the feathers. Pick off large clots of blood as best you can, but don't try to rub the blood off; this only smears it into the feathers. Carry the bird from the woods in a tote bag or game bag, taking special precautions to protect the tail feathers.

If you're having the entire bird mounted, it's best to freeze the carcass, unless you can get the bird to the taxidermist's shop immediately. To freeze the bird, wrap the head and neck in several layers of damp paper towel, and tuck the head under a wing. Wrap the entire body, except for the tail, in several layers of newspaper, taped tightly. Lay the carcass on a piece of stiff cardboard long enough to extend an inch or two past the longest tail feathers, then secure the body to the cardboard by wrapping tape around it. Place the wrapped turkey in a large cooler or cardboard box suitable for transporting, and freeze it solid. A turkey wrapped and frozen this way will remain frozen for two to four days at room temperature.

Inexpensive alternatives to a full body mount are do-it-yourself mounts of the legs, wings or beard (following pages).

HOW TO PREPARE AND MOUNT A TAIL

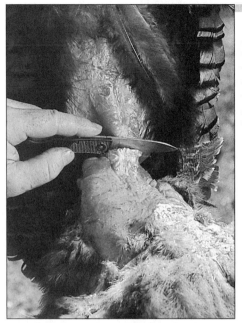

1. HANG the gobbler from the neck, and cut the tail off at the tailbone. Save as many rump feathers as you want by skinning up the back.

2. REMOVE the large pieces of meat from the base of the tail feathers with a sharp knife. The tailbone can also be snipped off using a wire cutter.

3. USE a knife to remove fat around and between the feather quills. NOTE: Oil glands at the base of the tail should also be removed (arrows).

4. APPLY a generous amount of salt or borax to the skin and the base of the tail. Allow the salt to draw excess oils for 8 to 12 hours.

(continued on next page)

(continued) HOW TO PREPARE AND MOUNT A TAIL

5. BRUSH off the oil-saturated salt, and rub new salt onto the skin and quills. This will remove any remaining fat and oil.

6. POSITION the tail flat on a large piece of cardboard or Styrofoam. Spread it open as you want it to appear. Pin into position. Use heavy books to hold the tail in place as it dries for several days.

174

7. USE a large pin to manipulate feathers into place. Try to hide any bent or broken feathers behind good ones. Frayed tips can be improved by wetting fingers and mending together.

8. COVER tail quills by using plaques (right), leather, metal, photographs or other turkey feathers glued in place (left).

175

HOW TO PRESERVE AND DISPLAY A BEARD

2. GRASP the base of the beard between the thumb and forefinger. Feel for the hard lump where the beard attaches to the skin. Cut the skin behind this base, and trim off excess meat and skin.

3. APPLY borax to the cleaned base, and allow to sit for 8 to 12 hours. Beards can be hung beneath a tail mount, displayed on a multibeard board, framed with a trophy spur or stuck in a hatband.

HOW TO PRESERVE LEGS

1. REMOVE legs at the knee joint with a sharp knife. Do not cut through any bone.

2. USE a bone saw or hacksaw to remove the middle joint of the leg, exposing the bone marrow.

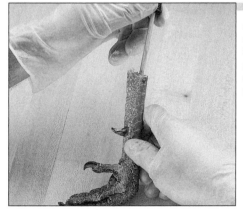

3. POKE with a wire or small screwdriver to remove bone marrow. Soak feet in a saturated saltwater solution.

HOW TO PRESERVE AND DISPLAY SPURS

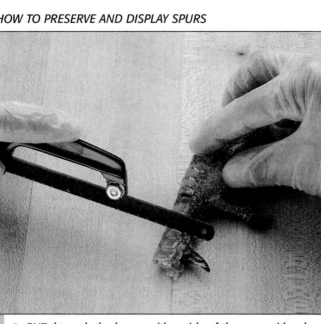

1. CUT through the leg on either side of the spur with a hacksaw or bone saw.

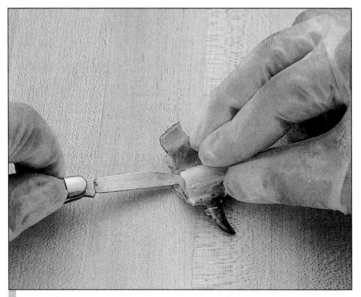

2. PEEL skin from the bone with a sharp knife. Clean out marrow with a small screwdriver.

178

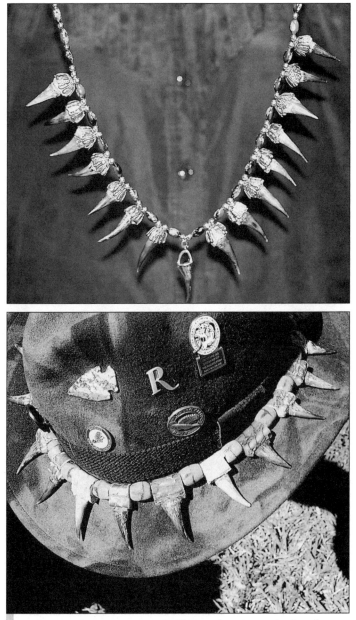

3. DISPLAY leg spurs on a necklace (above) or a hatband (below). They can also be put on keychains, call lanyards or tail fan mounts.

HOW TO PRESERVE A WING

1. DETACH the wing at the first joint by cutting through the knuckle area.

2. CUT along the entire underside of the wing, and peel back skin to expose the bone and flesh. Use a sharp knife to remove all meat from around bones.

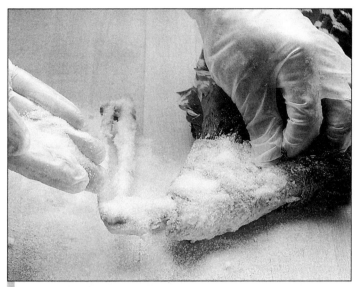

3. PEEL the skin all the way back and salt the skin and bone area, to remove all oils. After 8 to 12 hours, remove all oil-soaked salt and apply fresh salt.

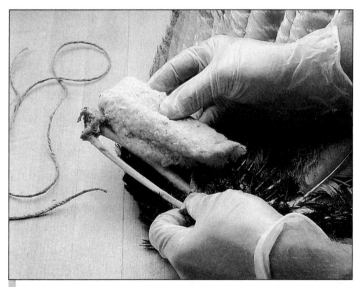

4. PACK cotton around the exposed bones to replace meat, tie into place with string and pull skin back over bones. Place the wing in desired position, and let dry.

181

Dressing &
Cooking Wild
Turkey

Field-dressing – removing the bird's entrails and crop immediately after the kill – isn't necessary if you are able to dress the bird fully within 1 hour of shooting it. But if you can't get the bird refrigerated within an hour, field-dress it immediately after photographing it.

To field-dress a wild turkey, cut the skin just below the pointed end of the breast, near the vent. Don't cut too deep, or you'll puncture the intestines. Reach in and pull out the entrails. If you like giblets, cut the heart, liver and gizzard free, and store them in a resealable plastic bag.

Next, remove the crop where the neck joins the breast. If the bird ate recently, the crop will be firm and roughly the size of a tennis ball. Cut through the breast skin to remove it and the esophagus attached to it.

Refrigerate, put the carcass on ice, or complete dressing it as soon as possible. If you plan to bake or smoke your bird, it is best to pluck it, because the skin protects the meat from drying out. If you prefer grilling or frying the breast meat, simply skin the bird. Some hunters bone out the thighs and drumsticks, but most save these tougher cuts for soup stock.

PLUCKING. First, cut off the beard and tail if you wish to save them. Then scald the bird to loosen its feathers. Add 1 tablespoon of dishwashing soap to 2 or 3 gallons of boiling water. Hold the turkey by its legs over a large tub, and pour the boiling water over the carcass, a little at a time. When the tub has sufficient water in it, dip the carcass and let the water work into all dry areas – but don't allow the bird to sit in the water and cook.

Test by pulling on the wing feathers, which are hardest to remove. If they easily pull out, the entire bird is ready to pluck. Pluck only a few feathers at a time to avoid tearing the skin. If the skin tears easily, you have probably "over-cooked" the bird during the scalding process. With practice, you'll develop a feel for just how long to scald the carcass before plucking.

After plucking, cut off the lower legs, the head and the neck. Do not remove the excess fatty breast tissue, common in adult gobblers; this fat helps keep the bird moist while cooking.

SKINNING & BREASTING. Slit the skin from tail to throat, and peel it away from the breast. Use a thin, long-bladed fillet knife to slice the meat away from each side of the breast bone. When finished, you should have two clean, boneless slabs of breast meat.

Recipes

ROASTED WILD TURKEY

Season the bird inside and out, and place in a cooking bag. Roast the bird at 325°F, approximately 15 minutes per pound. Birds are done when the temperature in the thickest part of the thigh reaches 185°F. Take care not to overcook, which can make meat tough and tasteless. A wild turkey can be roasted using the same recipe used for a store-bought domestic turkey, but decrease cooking time by about 20 percent.

SMOKED TURKEY

Although you can smoke a skinned turkey, a plucked bird gives better results. Simply place the turkey in the smoker and keep adding enough of your favorite wood chips to keep the container filled with smoke. Smoking a whole bird takes 6 to 12 hours – but the result is delicious. When smoking is completed, peel back the blackened skin and slice off slabs of moist breast meat.

FRIED TURKEY BREAST STRIPS

This method is a traditional favorite among turkey hunters. Begin by slicing the breast meat into strips about 1 inch wide. Soak these in a mixture of beaten egg and milk for 20 minutes. Put a cup of seasoned flour or pancake mix into a sturdy paper bag, drop in the turkey strips and shake to coat. Heat 1 inch of cooking oil in an electric fry pan or cast-iron skillet. When the oil is smoking hot, drop in the turkey strips; turn when lightly browned. To ensure tender, moist meat, don't overcook. Five to ten minutes should do it.

GRILLED TURKEY BREAST

Leave each half of the boned turkey breast intact. Lay the meat directly over hot coals, and season to taste. Grill only a few minutes on each side. Again, the secret is not to overcook; even a young jake will be tough as boot leather if you let it cook too long. As a variation, lay a strip or two of thick bacon over each breast while grilling to keep them moist and add flavor.

INDEX

A

Acorns in Turkey Diet, 23, 25
Aerial Photos, 95
Afternoon Hunting, 118, 150
Age of Turkeys, 20-22
  Breeding age, 22
  Determining, 8, 21, 22
  Distinguishing jake from mature
    bird, 21
Agricultural Damage by Turkeys, 23
Aiming Point, 42, 56, 57, 107, 121,
  122
  Setting up for the shot, 119-122
Alarm Calls by Turkeys, 35
Ambushing Gobbler with Hens, 154,
  155, 157
Ammunition,
  Muzzleloader, 49, 50
  Rifle, 53
  Shotgun, 44, 47 (chart)
Appearance, see: Description of
  Turkeys
Apprentice Jakes, 33
Archery, 54-57
  How to draw a bow on a turkey, 122
  Setting up for the shot, 119-122
  Shot placement, 56, 57, 122

B

Beard, 8, 9
  Length, 8, 22
  Multiple, 22
  Preserving & displaying, 176
Binoculars, Choosing, 123
Blinds & Blind Hunting, 55, 58-60,
  116, 162
Boat for Float-Hunting, 130, 133
  Soundproofing, 132
Boots & Footwear, 64, 65
Bows & Arrows, 54-57, 122
Box Calls, 75-77
  Protecting in rainy weather, 76, 158
Breasting Turkey, 184
Breeding, 20, 28-31
  Age of sexual maturity, 22

Breeding success, 20, 39
Displays & appearance, 8, 9, 30,
  102, 114
Fighting between toms, 33, 34
Nesting behavior, 30, 31
Vocalizations, 8, 9, 28-30, 33, 34,
  102

C

Cackling, Imitating with Calls, 77
Calling Turkeys, 72-91
  Air-activated calls, about, 84-88
  Calling hung-up gobbler, 140-143
  Calling to hens, 153, 154
  Call-shy turkeys, 148-151
  Creating "talking" decoy, 79
  Friction calls, 75-83
  Locator calls, 89-91
  Loud calling, 149
  Protecting calls in rainy weather, 76,
    158
  Specific sounds to imitate, 34, 35
  Voice calling, 74
  When to call, 30, 112-115, 124, 129,
    145, 153, 161, 162
  When to use various types, 55, 89,
    90, 99, 112-118, 131, 142, 145,
    149, 154, 161, 162
  See also: Vocalizations of Turkeys
Camouflage,
  Clothing, 66-68
  On weapon, 44, 55
Caruncles, 8, 9
Choke,
  On muzzleloader, 48, 49
  On shotgun, 43, 44
  Shot pattern effectiveness, 46
Clear-Cut Areas, 39
Clothing, 64-67
Clucking, 9, 160
  Imitating with calls, 76, 78, 80, 83,
    86, 87
  When to cluck, 55, 145, 149, 162
Cold Weather & Turkey Activity, 114,
  156
  See also: Winter

CREDITS

Contributing Photographers *(Note: T=Top, C=Center, B=Bottom, L=Left, R=Right, i=inset)*

Scott Anderson
Eden Prairie, Minnesota
©Scott Anderson: p. 60BL

Mike Biggs
Fort Worth, Texas
©Mike Biggs: pp. 9, 56-#2, 100C, 144-145, 156, 163T

Gary Clancy
Byron, Minnesota
©Gary Clancy: pp. 125T, 159

Dembinsky Photo Associates
Owosso, Michigan
©Carl R. Sams II: pp. 28-29

Laurie Lee Dovey
Alpharetta, Georgia
©Laurie Lee Dovey: p. 163B

Jeanne Drake
Las Vegas, Nevada
©Jeanne Drake: pp. 18B, 57-#4, 61

Gary W. Griffen
Red Hook, New York
©Gary W. Griffen: pp. 99T, 158B, 160-161

Donald M. Jones
Troy, Montana
©Donald M. Jones: pp. 14-15, 24, 32, 56-#3, 57-#5, 100B, 110-111, 146B, 152-153

Mitch Kezar
kezarphoto.com
©Mitch Kezar: p. 54

Bill Kinney
BillKinney.com
©Bill Kinney: p. 21

Lee Kline
Loveland, Colorado
©Lee Kline: pp. 6-7, 60T

Lance Krueger
McAllen, Texas
©Lance Krueger: cover-turkey, p. 148

Wyman Meinzer
Benjamin, Texas
©Wyman Meinzer: pp. 26, 34, 56-#1, 57-#6, 100T, 103

Gary Nelson
Altura, Minnesota
©Gary Nelson: p. 36

Bill Thomas
Missoula, Montana
©Bill Thomas: p. 19T

Lovett Williams
Cedar Key, Florida
©Lovett Williams: pp. 17, 19T

Gary Zahm
Los Banos, California
©Gary Zahm: p. 98T, 98i

Contributing Manufacturers

Cabela's – World's Foremost Outfitter
812 13th Avenue
Sidney, Nebraska 69160

Hunter's Specialties, Inc.
6000 Huntington Court N.E.
Cedar Rapids, Iowa 52402

Mossy Oak
P.O. Box 757
West Point, Mississippi 39773

Outland Sports
4500 Doniphan Drive
Neosho, Missouri 64850

Primos, Inc.
P.O. Box 12785
Jackson, Mississippi 39236

Realtree Products
1390 Box Circle
Columbus, Georgia 31907

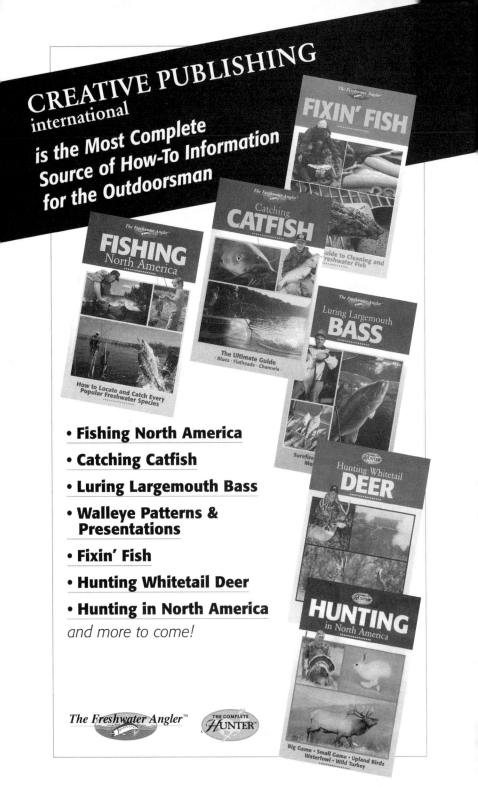